THE
STAR ANISE
CAFÉ
COOK BOOK

THE
STAR ANISE CAFÉ
COOK BOOK

VEGETARIAN WHOLEFOOD CUISINE

Nicholas Allan
&
Rahel Steffen

ASPECT DESIGN

The Star Anise Café Cook Book
Nicholas Allan and Rahel Steffen

Published by Aspect Design 2011
Malvern, Worcestershire, United Kingdom.

Printed by Butler Tanner & Dennis
Caxton Road, Frome, Somerset BA11 1NF United Kingdom
Tel: 01373 451500
E-mail: info@butlertanneranddennis.com
www.butlertanneranddennis.com

Star Anise Arts Café at the Painswick Inn
1 Gloucester Street, Stroud, GL5 1QG

www.staraniseartscafe.com

Illustrations by Selina Snow
Photography by Neil Speakman
Design by Ant Beetlestone
Cover and Typographical artwork by Dennis Gould
Layout by IKON Designs

CONTENTS

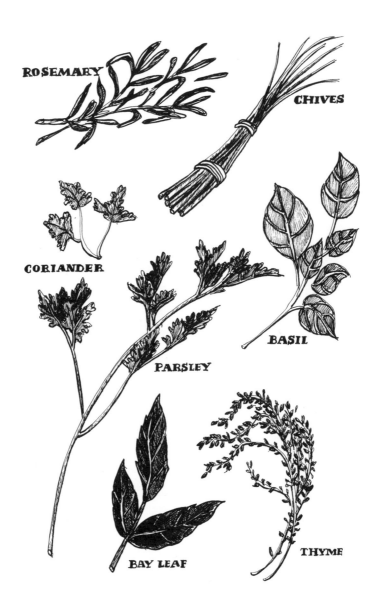

ROSEMARY

CHIVES

CORIANDER

BASIL

PARSLEY

BAY LEAF

THYME

INTRODUCTION

CHOOSING GOOD INGREDIENTS and cooking our own food is one of the most powerful things that we can do for ourselves. It gives us the chance to take responsibility for our health and general wellbeing in a very real sense, every day. We invest a lot of time and money in other areas of our lives, compared with what we put into choosing and preparing our food. It often goes unnoticed, how profoundly our way of life is affected by what we eat, even though we know that diet contributes to many problems to do with our health and levels of energy. Some of these problems could be eased, or avoided, by investing a little more in our food.

But cooking and work don't mix well. Caught up in our busy lives, it can be hard to see cooking as an enjoyable part of everyday life. Cooking in a café kitchen is no different – it can be just as much of a chore as it is at home. So it is important to keep things interesting and feel engaged with what we are doing. This doesn't always mean searching for new recipes and coming up with new dishes to make. More often than not, it just means giving over a little more of our time and energy to the kinds of things that we make anyway. Sometimes, it makes all the difference to cook something from scratch, rather than take the usual shortcuts. There is a lot of pleasure to be had from making something familiar and making it well.

It takes thought and skill to make food that is nourishing, wholesome and liked by whoever it is that we are cooking for (be it family, friends, or a large gathering). This is especially so if we rely less on meat and dairy products. There is an expectation that vegetarian food (or any food that is in some way curbed by dietary needs or preferences) is less tasty, less satisfying and somehow second best. Vegetarian food has to be very good and exceed expectations, if it is to cut through the myths. This is a challenge we face every day at the café. On the one hand, we wish to make nourishing vegetarian food, with little or no dairy products, eggs or refined sugar. But on the other, we need to make food that people like.

What works for us is an approach based on the ideas of wholefood and macrobiotic cooking and tempered by good common sense. We take inspiration from the lightness, colour and intense flavours of Southern European and Far Eastern cooking traditions. Our menu is a lucky dip of familiar favourites, prepared with a wide array of vegetables and fresh produce. Some of our cooking methods might be unfamiliar and take more time, but we use them because they help to conserve the goodness and flavours, naturally present in the food.

We hope that this book may be useful and inspiring, for all those who wish to have more of a say in the food we eat. If we can encourage a few people to try out something they haven't come across before, then so much the better.

At the heart of good cooking is the excitement and delight that comes with trying something out for the first time…

Nicholas Allan

About Star Anise Arts Café

STAR ANISE ARTS CAFÉ is one of those places that feels like it has been there for ages. A short distance from the town centre in Stroud, Gloucestershire, the café is tucked away among the buildings of the Painswick Inn. It shares an old stone archway and courtyard with a host of different ventures also housed within the same buildings, including theatre projects, craft workshops, a bakery and a Kindergarten.

When it gets busy and the weather is warm, the café spills out onto the courtyard. Sometimes the place becomes a venue for live music, exhibitions, storytelling and speakers. But more usually, it ebbs and flows with people stopping by for a coffee, friends or colleagues meeting up for lunch, parents with children settling down on the sofa for a couple of hours, on a quiet afternoon.

The kitchen is in full view of the café. Anyone who happens to be looking, at any given time, might notice snatches of the on-going drama of cooking. The ever-repeating sequence of preparing and chopping vegetables, measuring ingredients, stirring pots and pans, putting trays into the oven, serving food onto plates, washing up and cleaning down. Each part of the process is as important as the next. In our effort to make food that is both nourishing and delicious, our way of working mirrors home cooking at its best.

LAUNCHED IN 2004, THE CAFÉ owes a great deal to the hard work and strong ideals of its founders, Nicholas Allan, Milda Gudelyte and Alexandra Hoppe. The three met whilst training at the Concord School of Culinary Arts in London. For Nicholas, the approach he encountered there was inspirational. The school has its roots in

wholefoods and macrobiotic cooking and remains an important reference point for the café, to this day. Its influence can be seen in the consistent use of grains, the attention given over to the preparation of fruit and vegetables and how different foods are combined.

It took a leap of faith, lots of courage and a somewhat vague business plan to get Star Anise off the ground. Despite a slightly shaky grasp of how to work the new coffee machine, the first day of opening saw the café filled to capacity with well-wishing friends and customers.

Over the next few weeks, Star Anise began to find its feet and the menu and day-to-day routines gradually fell into place. Everyone involved was amazed when, a month later, they were forced to take on new staff to cope with the demand. The café has proved popular ever since and has carved a place for itself as the meeting place of choice for a very loyal and eclectic bunch of people.

How we cook

So OFTEN, AT HOME, cooking is a rushed affair. Dirty dishes and muddy vegetables fight it out for space in the sink and peelings get strewn over the counter. Onions scorch in the pan and things get broken. Little wonder that it doesn't feel like much fun at times.

We are not immune to the occasional meltdown at the cafe, but in a professional kitchen, being organized makes all the difference to the general running of things. You don't want to find yourself dealing with lunch orders whilst knee-deep in washing up, or while your hands are welded to a sticky mass of rye sourdough. So we try to keep the different stages of the cooking process separate, as far as we can. This ensures that there is space, at the right time, for each task. It makes the whole thing much less stressful.

The cooking cycle, as we see it, is made up of different stages: planning, preparing, cooking, serving and clearing. Common sense; but it can be helpful, even for the most experienced cook, to stop and think about each stage of the cycle and re-acknowledge that they are all equally important – even washing up. In the end, it all has a bearing on how the food tastes and how nourishing it is.

PLANNING. Before even so much as picking up a pan, it helps to start with a clear idea of the finished dish. Taking into account what is available, how much time there is, the cost and who it is you are cooking for, picture in your mind's eye what the food will be like, when cooked and ready to serve. Think about all the different parts that make up the whole. This goes for whether you are using a recipe or not. Recipes can only ever give a very general outline of what to do – only you know exactly what you are up against. Sometimes, if there are lots of complex tasks or ingredients involved (like when cooking for large numbers, on a special occasion), making a list can be useful. Whether you do or you don't, the important thing is to hold on to the picture of the finished dish.

PREPARING. It is always a good thing to give over some time and attention to just preparing ingredients, before doing any cooking. Leaving the cooking till a little later means fewer difficult, chaotic moments. Start by getting together all the main ingredients that you need and measuring them out. In most cases, measuring by eye or by handful is all that is needed.

When cutting up fruit or vegetables, think about the kind of cuts you make, so that the shape and size of the pieces fit with the type of dish. At the café, we might make small neat dice for a delicate broth, or angular, chunky pieces for a winter stew. Make sure knives are sharp and give chopping boards plenty of room. Have ready a bowl or pan to collect the prepared fruit or vegetables (a 'receiving bowl', as we call it) and also something like a colander, to catch the peelings and off-cuts. If children are helping out, this is especially important, otherwise you can tie yourself into knots in a small kitchen. Clear up as you go along, making way for each new task.

COOKING. In an ideal world, cooking only starts once all the preparation is done. In reality, this isn't usually the case, but it is something worth aiming for. The reason for keeping the preparation and cooking stages separate is that they each need a different kind of focus. Cooking is about good judgment and timing, about engaging with the food as it cooks and being aware of how it is changing. Whereas with preparation, the focus is on sorting through and organising ingredients and having them ready for later (*mis en place*, as we call it).

Being sensitive to seasoning is a big part of being able to cook well. Salt is only one dimension of seasoning, since good flavour develops from a balance of salty, sweet, sour, bitter and savoury flavours. A soup or sauce, which is somehow lacking in flavour, might need to be more sour, or sweet, rather than simply more salty; or it might need to have a stronger savoury base flavour.

Being aware of timing is important too. It is surprisingly hard to stay conscious of things that are out of sight, whether behind oven doors or under a saucepan lid. Checking things often, cooking things slowly over a very low heat, using a timer when baking – all these can help avoid surprises.

Every now and then, it is good to go back to the picture of the finished dish. Even though it might not be completely clear and specific details carry on emerging as you go along, keep it in mind.

SERVING. By now you should have all the elements (including perhaps a few unexpected and unplanned ones) to make up the finished dish. When cooking for large numbers, the skill is in guiding all the different parts of the meal so that they all come together at the same point. The more organized and unhurried this is, the less stressful the atmosphere in the kitchen and the better the quality of the food. Make a habit of checking the seasoning just before serving the food. In our kitchen, this is a key moment, because once missed, it can mean that a dish is served in a way that was not intended.

In the café, placing the food on the plate is the most 'painterly' part of the cooking process. We try to arrange the food as simply and beautifully as possible, paying attention to detail, but avoiding presentation for presentation's sake. First impressions count and the picture of the plate is what people see first.

At home, presentation is less about the picture of the plate, except perhaps when cooking for special occasions and friendly get-togethers. But anyone cooking for children will recognise that it takes some cunning to serve up 'healthy' food. Presentation, in this case, is more about finding ways of arranging the food so that it appeals, such as serving vegetables separately, or putting soup into small ramekins.

CLEANING DOWN. As we see it, cleaning is just as important as preparing, cooking and serving food. We don't always manage to live up to this idea, but things tend to go more smoothly when we keep on top of the cleaning. As well as general cleaning, this means clearing away as we are working (a principle that is instilled into every chef, throughout their training). Putting ingredients away and washing up as we go along, makes for a calm space and less problems. And allowing time for a proper 'clean down' right at the end (finishing off the washing up, wiping down the surfaces and returning things to their place) makes it easier to start cooking again, next time. This can't be emphasized enough and is of course essential in the café.

The kitchen cupboard

ONE OF THE BIG DIFFERENCES between cooking at home and cooking in a café kitchen, is the size of the kitchen store cupboard. Cooking for large numbers has its advantages; we can buy in a much wider variety of ingredients, like fresh fruit and vegetables, without fear of them going off before they have been used up. At home, what there is to hand tends to be more limited. Making anything out of the ordinary usually involves doing some shopping first, which can be off-putting.

Having said all that, there is very little that we use in our kitchen, that you can't get hold of from a supermarket, market stall or health food shop. The recipes in this book take into account that you probably won't have four or five types of vinegar in your cupboard, or a plentiful supply of pine-nuts that you can afford to measure out by the handful. But there are a few unusual ingredients that we use, which might be unfamiliar, but which are worth getting hold of, as they bring some unique qualities and flavours to the food we make and give it its 'Star Anise' character.

KOMBU (OR KELP). This is a type of seaweed, used widely in Japanese cooking. It comes in a dried form, as thin sheets. We use it for adding goodness and depth of flavour to vegetable stock. Kombu also has tenderising properties and can be added to the pot when cooking beans and pulses, so as to soften them. It is rich in minerals, particularly iron and is available from Chinese supermarkets and health food shops.

TAMARI AND SOY SAUCE (SHOYU). Soy sauce (shoyu) is traditionally made from fermented soya beans and wheat and is an essential ingredient of wholefood cooking. Tamari is similar in essence to soy sauce, but is much saltier and contains no wheat gluten. It gives a depth of flavour to dishes and is usually added right at the end of the cooking process and with care, due to its potency. It is worth noting that good quality soy sauce or tamari are much more concentrated and potent in flavour than cheaper supermarket imitations. These tend to be made with lots of salt, caramelised sugar and water. Real tamari and soy sauce are made using techniques that preserve the goodness of the soya beans and transform them into something that is more easily digestible.

UMIBOSHI. A paste made from sour plums, umiboshi is used in Japanese cooking as a seasoning, to add a tangy, salty flavour. It also has powerful medicinal properties, as it is strongly alkaline and works to counter-balance more acidic foods. We use umiboshi for marinades, relishes and add it to sautéed greens. It can be bought in small jars from healthfood shops and some supermarkets.

MISO. Miso is a Japanese stock paste made from fermented soya beans and some form of grain, such as rice or barley. We use it mainly in soups, to enhance the savoury base flavour. When using miso, it is important to add it at the end of the cooking process, when the soup is no longer boiling. This way, all the goodness and the enzymes in the miso are preserved. Miso is available in health

11

food shops and some supermarkets. White miso is sweeter, milder and lighter in colour and is more accessible for younger palates. It is harder to get hold of, but can be found in specialist Japanese food shops and some healthfood shops.

TOFU. Soya bean curd, or tofu, is familiar to many as a vegetarian source of protein. It comes in different varieties and more recently, different flavours. Silken tofu is smooth and delicate and is often used in wholefood cooking for deserts and sauces. The type of tofu used for general cooking is more robust and can be grilled, fried, used in salads, stews and oven bakes. As well as plain tofu, there is herbed tofu, smoked tofu (which we use a lot), tofu rosso (it has sun-dried tomato in it) among others. Plain tofu is only as interesting as the flavours around it and is enhanced by something like a spicy ginger, mirin and tamari marinade.

MIRIN. A sweet Japanese seasoning, made from rice wine, we add mirin to sautéed vegetables, clear noodle soups, relishes and stir-fries. In Japanese cooking, mirin is always added before tamari or soy sauce (shoyu) – 'sweet before salt' – as it is understood that this gives the food a more balanced flavour.

DRIED MUSHROOMS. These can add deep flavour and a rich, dark colour to all kinds of dishes, from soups, sauces and gravy, to oven bakes and stir-fries. Dried mushrooms need to be rehydrated, either by simmering them in a pan of water, or by immersing them in boiling water and leaving them to soak for half an hour or so. Alternatively, they can be added dry, as long as there is plenty of liquid for them to soak up – like when making vegetable stock, for instance. Shitake and porcini mushrooms are the most commonly available dried mushrooms and can be bought in supermarkets or health-food shops. Other wild mushrooms can also be found on market stalls and in smaller, more specialist shops.

FRESH HERBS. Fresh herbs can make a vast difference to the quality of a dish. But they are often left off the shopping list because of the way they are sold (small quantities that are expensive and over-packaged, or pots of fragile herbs that quickly wilt). If you don't grow your own, it makes more sense to buy them from a green grocers or market stall, where they are often sold loose, so that you can choose the quantity that you need. Thyme is a much under-used herb, which we like to add to savoury stews, sauces and one-pots, for its earthy, savoury flavour. Rosemary and bay leaves are useful in this way, too. Other herbs that we use everyday are basil, parsley, coriander, chervil, mint and chives.

CULINARY OILS. We need oil as part of a balanced diet and it is important not to scrimp on quality when it comes to choosing oil. A good oil helps to carry the flavours of other ingredients in a dish, making them richer and more vivid. When using oils, it helps to match the oil to the dish. Roughly speaking, we tend to use olive oil for European and Mediterranean-style dishes, whereas we use sesame oil for Oriental-inspired dishes. Don't be afraid of mixing a stronger oil with a more neutral-flavoured one, like sunflower oil. We use light oils, like sunflower oil, in place of butter or margarine in baking, as an alternative to dairy products.

13

INTRODUCTION

SPELT FLOUR. Spelt flour is milled from an old variety of wheat and can be bought as either white or wholemeal spelt flour. It works well as a wheat flour substitute in baking, especially for pastry and cookies. We use spelt flour in many of our cookies, for its nutty flavour and short texture. It is more expensive than wheat flour, but it is readily available from supermarkets and health food shops.

AGAVE SYRUP (OR AGAVE NECTAR). Made from the sap of a cactus plant native to the tropical regions of Central America, agave is a light, fluid syrup, with a delicate flavour. It works well instead of sugar in baking, though mixtures are much more liquid than when made in the normal way with sugar. Buy organic agave syrup if possible, as it tends to be less highly refined. Available by the jar, like honey, from health food shops.

RICE SYRUP AND RICE MALT SYRUP. Rice and other grain-based syrups are slightly thicker than agave syrup, but work equally well as a sugar substitute in baking and general cooking. It is worth noting that rice syrup is gluten-free, but rice malt syrup is not, as it is malted with barley and barley contains gluten. Rice syrup and rice malt syrup are available by the jar, from health food shops.

BARLEY MALT SYRUP. With its robust, malty flavour and toffee-like texture, barley malt is best used in combination with other forms of sweetener in baking. Otherwise, it can tend to take over and make the final result dark-coloured and dense. It works best when it makes up about a quarter of the total amount of syrup, in cakes like chocolate cake, carrot cake and in some of the darker, nuttier cookies. Barley malt syrup also gives a more rounded taste to home-made bread, such as wholemeal bread, or sourdough bread.

MAPLE SYRUP. Expensive but delicious, maple syrup can be used for more than just pancakes – it livens up marinades and dressings, caramelised onions, roasted vegetables and toasted seeds. In baking, use it sparingly in combination with agave or rice syrup, to give added flavour to cakes and cookies.

The 'magic four' base ingredients

ONION, CELERY, CARROT AND LEEK are the magic four, the bedrock of many of our dishes. Leek is not always available when it is out of season, but the other three are almost always easy to get hold of, all year round. In cooking this way, we are drawing on classical French cooking, where sautéing some onion, celery and carrot is the starting point for a wide range of dishes, from soups to casseroles and sauces.

The reason for using the 'magic four' is that it helps develop a good, balanced base flavour – it literally lays the foundations for a dish. If the onion and leek are cooked slowly and gently, with some salt added, to draw out the juices, they turn buttery soft and start to caramelise. Against the caramelised onion and leek, you have the clean, herby flavour of celery and the earthy, bittersweet flavour of carrot. Together, they are a near-perfect balance of sweet, sour, salty, bitter and savoury flavours. The mixture also incorporates both warming and cooling food types – carrot is a 'warming' type of food, whereas celery is more 'cooling'.

Perhaps the most important thing about the 'magic four' is that they give consistency to the flavour of our food. No matter which other ingredients are added afterwards, this base is still there, like a quiet, familiar presence in the background.

Tomato in everything

FOR SOME REASON, tomato has come to feature very heavily in vegetarian cooking and in our food culture in general. Until fairly recently, tomato was something of a rarity, appearing when it was in season, like strawberries. Over the past few decades, our love affair with South European and Mediterranean cuisine has changed our relationship with the tomato and now we use it all the time. Fresh, tinned, sun-dried; as passata, puree, salsa and ketchup – the tomato has crept into everything and become completely indispensable.

The problem with tomato is that it is not easy on the digestive system, being very acidic. In food cultures where tomato is used a lot, it is also understood that the fruit needs to be well ripened and cooked slowly over a long period of time, to make it more digestible. Having cherry picked the tomato, we seem to have discarded the knowledge of how to prepare it.

At the café, we try to use tomato as sparingly as possible. Rather than reaching for the tin of tomatoes to pack out a casserole, we prefer to make use of the juices released by the vegetables during cooking. Liquid can be thickened with arrowroot, or by blending a portion of the vegetables and then returning the puree to the pot. We use ingredients such as miso, yeast extract, dried mushrooms, as well as fresh herbs like thyme, to give our dishes that strong, sweet-savoury quality, which tomatoes are able to give. And as for colour,

16

if tomato red isn't the overriding colour of a dish, other ingredients get a chance to shine and the dish often looks more complex and interesting.

Cow's milk

DAIRY PRODUCTS, for many people, are a vital part of any vegetarian meal. Relying on dairy products is understandable, as it has always had a strong place in our food culture. But more and more people are turning away from dairy. For some people, this is because of lactose intolerance. For others, it is because they are worried about the health effects of dairy products. Cattle farming methods today are far from ideal, with hormones and antibiotics finding their way into the food we eat.

There is a strong need for taking stock of how we use dairy products and finding other ways of cooking, so that it is used more sparingly. In our kitchen, we try to keep dairy products to a minimum. We prefer to make dishes which don't rely too heavily on butter, milk and cheese; dishes based instead on vegetables and grains, nuts, seeds and beans. Wherever possible, we try to substitute dairy products with dairy-free alternatives. Cow's milk is swapped for soya, rice or oat milk and butter for olive oil or dairy-free margarine. If cheese is an important part of the dish, we prefer to use goats or sheep's milk cheese, or swap it for other forms of vegetarian protein. In the end, we try to treat dairy products as a form of 'seasoning', as something to add sparkle to a dish that is all but complete, with or without it.

What makes a meal?

IF WE BREAK AWAY from the idea that a meal is structured around some form of protein, as in the traditional 'meat and two vegetables' model, we need another way of thinking about the parts that make up the meal as a whole. In our kitchen, we think of a meal as being made up of five elements, any of which can be the focus of the meal. These five elements are loosely linked to major food groups. Referring to them helps to ensure a balance of warming and cooling foods, protein, minerals, flavours and textures.

Planning a meal is about finding the springboard, the most inspiring starting point and building the meal around it. This might be something that needs using up, something you haven't had for a while, or something that is in season and at its peak, such as asparagus, or some flaky-skinned new potatoes. Make recipes work for you rather than the other way round. Pinch the basic idea, but temper it with your own knowledge.

THE GRAIN (OR CARBOHYDRATE). This tends to be the default starting point, when planning a meal that is not structured around the protein. We cook with rice a lot at the café; long-grain or short-grain brown rice is often the basis for our dish of the day. In macrobiotic cooking, rice is held to be neither excessively 'warming', nor 'cooling' and therefore a well-balanced source of nourishment. Apart from rice, we use wheat, in the form of pasta, bread, pastry and other baked goods. But it is good to interchange rice and wheat with other grains, to bring in more variety and support health. Oats and barley are natively grown grains and are very versatile. Gluten-free grains include millet, corn and quinoa. Potato, though not a grain, is naturally also gluten-free. It is worth noting that the grain need not be the main focus of the meal, it can be anything from a crispy piece of grilled polenta to go with a spicy one-pot, to an oat pastry crust for a flan.

PROTEIN. Leaving aside animal-derived protein, this group includes beans, lentils, nuts, seeds and tofu. The best vegetarian meals include one or more of these ingredients, but quite sparingly – they are rich foods, that take some work to digest and we don't, on the whole, need to eat as much as we think we do. Wherever possible, let the vegetables and grains occupy the centre-ground of a meal, so that the protein becomes an integral part of the meal, but no longer the feature.

ROOT VEGETABLES AND GOURDS. These vegetables are sweet and starchy. They are warming, wintry foods and include carrots, parsnips, squashes and sweet potatoes. In Chinese medicine, it is understood that these foods need to be included in the diet, in some way, even in the heat of the summer months, as they help prepare the body for the coming winter. Whether you believe in this or not, there is no doubt that they help to underpin a meal and give food a comforting quality.

LEAFY GREENS. If root vegetables and gourds are warming, leafy greens have a cooling quality. They include winter greens like kale and cabbages and summer vegetables like salad leaves, spinach and fresh herbs. Sorely under-represented on our table, we don't tend to eat as much leafy greens as we should. It is a food group rich in iron, calcium and other important minerals. These minerals help

19

to support those organs in our body, which govern our vitality (in particular, the kidneys). So the more leafy greens we can include, the better.

A SAUCE (OR GRAVY, SALSA, RELISH, OR PICKLE). This can take different forms, depending on the dish. A sauce can be part of the main dish, as it is in a casserole or one-pot, where it is the stock, or gravy and 'carries' the vegetables and protein. Or it can be a spicy addition on the side, livening up the more muted flavours of grains and vegetables. Either way, it makes the meal more palatable, by bringing fluid and flavour to the dish – it is often the sauce or relish that brings all the other elements together and defines the dish.

The concept of 'Umami'

UMAMI is a Japanese term which is best translated as 'savouriness'. Umami is about more than the seasoning, it is the underlying, savoury base flavour in a dish. A meal that combines all five of the basic elements (grain, protein, root vegetable, leafy greens and sauce) and has a good, savoury base flavour, shouldn't seem to be lacking in anything. It should stand up on its own, without the need for meat or dairy products.

The secret is to work with your ingredients, preparing them in ways that add depth of flavour. This can be achieved in many different ways and doesn't necessarily mean resorting to an arsenal of strong spices (guaranteed to put off many younger children). It is about establishing a good, savoury base, using a flavoursome stock, or the 'magic four' ingredients (onion, leek, celery and carrot). It involves working with chopped fresh herbs, dried mushrooms and seasonings like tamari, mirin and miso. It is about using long, slow cooking techniques that conserve natural goodness and flavour. Time and time again, we have found that this way of cooking has helped our food to be liked and accepted, even by the more conservative among us.

Tricks of the trade

THE WAY WE WORK at the café – our cooking approach – is just as important as the ingredients we use and how we pair them together. We always try to give some thought to the size and shape of the cut, when preparing ingredients, so that they 'sit' nicely together and suit a particular dish. The cooking methods we use preserve these shapes and as far as possible try to conserve the goodness naturally present in the food.

Knife work

One of the easiest ways of notching up the quality of a dish is to cut the vegetables to suit what you are making. We are very used to the idea of cutting vegetables into dice, but square isn't always the best or most pleasing shape for a vegetable. Try to include a variety of more irregular cuts, slices and strips in your cooking and you will be surprised by how much it changes the food.

DICE. Diced vegetables can range from the very small, in a grain salad or salsa, to the very large, in a vegetable stew. Dice are at their best when kept small – if cutting vegetables for roasting or for stews, they almost always look better cut into more irregular shapes, like long, thick diagonal slices, strips, or chunky 'roll cut' pieces.

21

Roll cut. This kind of cut can be used for any long, narrow vegetable, like carrot, parsnip and so on. It is literally a case of slicing off a small chunk, on the diagonal, then rolling the vegetable over a little and slicing off another chunk. The irregular, pyramid-like shapes help the vegetables 'sit' well together in soups and stews, or anything where you might have lots of different vegetables nestling together. Cut this way, vegetables are more robust and able to withstand longer cooking times without falling apart.

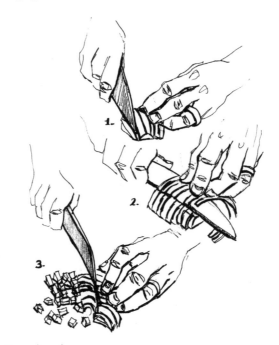

How to chop an onion.

IRREGULAR CHUNKS. This is like the roll cut, but used for vegetables which don't 'roll', such as squash, potato, peppers and so on. The idea is to break away from the squareness of diced pieces and cut pieces into more triangular or pyramid-like shapes.

SQUAT PENCIL CUT. One to use in soups, grain salads and one-pot dishes, where you want small pieces, but not dice. It can be used for any vegetable that can be cut into roughly pencil shaped strips. The strips are gathered together and sliced on the diagonal, so creating small shard-like pieces, rather than dice.

SLICES. Slices come in all sorts of shapes and can be cut straight or on the diagonal, thick and chunky, or paper thin. Slices work well where there is as little stirring or liquid involved in the cooking as possible, so that they don't over-cook or fall apart. Delicate broths or layered bakes are ideal, as are salads or pickled vegetables (such as radish).

STRIPS. Strips can be chunky for chips and roasted vegetables, or matchstick thin for salads and stir-fries. Like with slices, the less stirring and liquid involved in the cooking, the better.

Cooking methods

Cooking need not involve heat. When you crush a clove of garlic with salt, it 'cooks' the garlic slightly and takes off the raw edge. The same goes for marinating food in lemon juice or vinegar – pickling is a form of 'cooking', too. By cooking ingredients, it is believed that they become more digestible. On the other hand, overcooking can reduce the goodness in the food, making it dull and unpalatable. The skill is in treading a fine line between the two, cooking the food just enough, but not too much.

'DROP LID' METHOD. We use this method a lot, for cooking vegetables. It is a sort of braising technique, which is done on the stovetop rather than in the oven. It allows the vegetables to cook with hardly any need for added liquid – to steam in their own juices, in effect. This way, all the goodness in the vegetables is conserved and their flavours intensified. The 'drop lid' method works as easily at home as it does in a café kitchen. What you need is a large saucepan, ideally with a lid. Crucially, you need a second, smaller lid (or a piece of baking parchment), which fits snuggly inside the saucepan – the 'drop lid'. This sits directly on top of the vegetables and stops moisture from escaping. The main saucepan lid can be used as well if preferred; it keeps in the heat, thus creating a sort of stovetop 'oven'.

BLANCHING. Blanching is a way of cooking vegetables so that they loose as little goodness, flavour and colour as possible. The idea is to plunge the vegetables into boiling, salted water, so that they cook very quickly, but only very briefly. Once tender, the vegetables are lifted out of the water with a slotted spoon and cooled down rapidly, usually by running them under cold water. This way, they stay brightly coloured and retain a little of their raw crunchiness. At home, where quantities are much smaller, there is little call for a large pan of water, simmering away on the back of the stove, as there is in a commercial kitchen. Instead, half-fill a small saucepan with water, add a pinch of salt and bring it to the boil. Add the vegetables and cook them over a high heat, for a few minutes. Lift them out of the water with a slotted spoon (or drain them, using a colander). Cool them down, by spreading them out on a cold surface, such as a plate. Blanched vegetables can later be reheated by sautéing them, or adding them to a main pot of soup or stew, near the end of the cooking process. Alternatively, they can be used in flan fillings, salads and many other dishes.

PICKLING. We use pickling in its barest sense, as a way of 'cooking' finely cut vegetables with a dressing or marinade. Rather than embarking on a mission to fill our store-cupboard shelves with dusty, labelled jars, we make up a bit of something tart and crunchy once in a while, to go with a salad or main dish, or brighten up a sandwich. Sometimes, when the vegetables in question are harder or more earthy (red cabbage, for instance), we heat the marinade first and then work it into the vegetables whilst warm, so as to help them absorb it better. We also like to use Ume seasoning (a Japanese vinegar-alternative) for pickling, as it brings a unique sharp, salty taste. Other ingredients that we use are rice vinegar, lemon juice, white wine and cider vinegar and balsamic vinegar.

PRESSURE COOKING. Pressure cookers are not for everyone. It takes a while to get used to them and the hissing sounds they make can be unnerving. However, there is no denying how useful and efficient they can be. For cooking grains, dried beans and pulses, they are much more effective than normal cooking methods. If you get the timing about right and the amount of liquid just so, you will end up with perfectly cooked grains and pulses, that hold their shape and are completely tender inside.

It takes some trial and error to arrive at this stage and the chances are, that you might end up with a pan of mushy beans the first time around. This is because you won't be prepared for how quickly things cook in a pressure cooker. But persevere and you will get a feel for roughly how many minutes it takes to cook rice (about 5 minutes after the first whistle, for long grain brown rice) and chickpeas (about 20 minutes). Pretty much everything else falls somewhere in between. The timing for any grain or pulse depends on its size, as well as the quantity you are cooking. It also depends on how hard the grain or pulses are – if you have soaked them for several hours or overnight, the cooking time will be shorter than if they go into the pan dry.

Be sure to take good care of a pressure cooker, checking the fittings and tightening the valves regularly and giving it a good clean after use.

COOKING BEANS AND PULSES. Although it isn't indicated in the recipes, there are a few tricks that we use when cooking beans and pulses, to ensure that they are perfectly tender and full of flavour. Beans and chickpeas are usually soaked overnight and then drained and covered with plenty of fresh water. A piece of dried kombu (kelp) is added, to help tenderise the beans (and also because it adds minerals). The beans are then cooked in a pressure cooker, or simmered in a heavy-based pan, till tender. Lentils, on the other hand, are not soaked over night. They are put into a pan with a bay leaf and an unpeeled clove of garlic, which has been bashed with the flat of a knife, so as to release its juices. This helps to give the lentils more flavour, but is not essential. What is important is that beans and lentils are tender (as well as still completely intact), as they are notoriously difficult to digest, if they are not fully cooked.

Pressure cookers help to get to this point more quickly, but a long, slow simmering will also do the trick.

Thickening soups and sauces. Some of our thick soups are partially blended, by taking out a portion of the vegetables, blending it and returning it to the pot. This way, you have a thick base and the remaining vegetables still keep their well-defined shape, which they would lose if you were to give the pot a quick burst with a hand blender. It also means there is less call for flour and potato-rich bases, which can be heavy and override other flavours. We also use the thickener, arrowroot (similar to cornflour), for giving extra body to more delicate dishes, like sauces, one-pots and stir-fries.

Toasting nuts and seeds. Imagine putting dry bread in the toaster. The toast that pops up is crunchy, but also dry. Now imagine toasting a slice of fresh bread. When it comes up it is crisp on the outside, but still moist and tender inside. So it is with nuts and seeds. If you give them a rinse before toasting them (by running them under cold water, in a sieve), they will swell slightly and hold moisture, even when toasted. What you end up with are nuts and seeds that still have a roasted flavour, but are tender, rather than desiccated and hard.

Introduction

Making stock from scratch. Good vegetable stock can take a soup or a sauce to a completely different level, in terms of the depth of flavour it gives. In Japanese and indeed in French cooking, there are dozens of variations on the stock theme and one or the other version might be called upon, depending on the particular recipe in hand. We don't go this far in our kitchen, but we might emphasise a particular flavour, such as shitake mushroom or onion, or we might add some ginger or chili, depending on the kind of soup we wish to make.

At home, where time and ingredients are more limited, making fresh stock takes some organising, but it is still well worth the effort. Much like making bread, the actual time involved in preparing stock is quite small, after which it pretty much takes care of itself. It needn't involve a lot of different ingredients, either. The most basic Japanese stock, a simple 'Dashi', is made with only two ingredients: some dried shitake mushroom and a piece of kombu (kelp). These are simmered in a pan of water and impart a rich, deep colour and flavour, as well as lots of minerals. To make things easier, prepare a vegetable stock at the same time as cooking other dishes, rather than treating it as a separate task. Fresh stock can be stored in a container in the fridge or freezer, if it is not to be used straightaway.

Stock is like the lifeblood of cooking, like the ocean. It is where the real poetry of cooking lies. – Nicholas Allan

28

SOUP
OF THE DAY

SOUP OF THE DAY

THERE IS SOMETHING TIMELESS about soup. Stew is the ancestor of all cooking and is the ultimate one-pot meal: simple, nourishing and economical. It can be stretched to feed many and it is open to endless variation, according to what is available. As a symbol of sharing, there is nothing more democratic than eating from the same pot.

Soup and good bread makes for an easy, light meal. Since it keeps well, it can form the basis of several meals over the next few days, if you make enough. It can vary according to the time of year. When it's cold outside, you might want substantial, chunky soups of root vegetables and winter greens, or thick, densely-packed stews, with lentils or beans. In warmer weather, you might prefer delicate broths, with more liquid and the vegetables cut more finely.

A good soup needs a well-flavoured liquid to really sing. The quality of the stock is important and it is definitely worth making your own stock once in a while, if you are normally a stock-cube or bouillon user. Miso, a Japanese fermented stock paste, is an alternative to instant stock, as it adds natural goodness as well as a very distinctive, savoury taste. A splash of wine, if you like it, never goes amiss in a good broth and can do wonders for the flavour of a simple soup.

Soup doesn't on the whole need any dressing up, but once in a while, you might want to pull out the stops for a special occasion. Try topping soups with a spoonful of flavoursome oil, chopped fresh herbs, or a spicy pistou. Something like this can completely transform a humble soup, by adding a shot of vivid colour or a contrasting flavour and as a garnish, it has more impact than if it were cooked into the soup.

Vegetable stock

Dried mushrooms give our stock a rich dark colour and kombu naturally fortifies it with iron and minerals. But they are not essential – a simple stock can be made with just a handful of ingredients. Avoid using brassicas (like cabbage and broccoli) and anything too bitter, or strongly-coloured (like beetroot).

GF, V, DF

1 onion

1-2 cloves of garlic

1-2 stems of celery, plus any celery leaves

Any suitable, good-quality vegetable off-cuts *(leek greens, carrots, celeriac, courgette stalks and scrapings from the inside of squashes)*

Any spare herbs, or herb stalks *(parsley, thyme, basil)*

1 piece of kombu *(optional)*

A few pieces of dried mushroom

(shitake, porcini, mixed wild mushrooms)

Makes about 3 litres / 6 pints

PEEL THE ONION and cut it into quarters. Cut the garlic cloves in half, skin included. Chop the celery sticks in half. Put all the vegetables into a large pan, along with the herbs or herb stalks, dried mushrooms and the piece of kombu. Add about 3 litres / 6 pints of water, more or less, depending on the size of the pan and bring it to the boil. When almost boiling, turn down the heat and leave the stock to gently simmer, for an hour or so. Strain off the liquid and use it as needed, or store it in a container in the fridge, for later use.

Simple summer vegetable broth

There is nothing more sophisticated than a good broth, with beautifully cut vegetables suspended in a well-flavoured liquid.

GF, V, DF

1 onion

1 leek

2-3 carrots

2 stems of celery

1 small courgette *(green or yellow)*

A handful of green beans

3-4 tbsp peas *(fresh or frozen)*

1 litre / 2 pints of vegetable stock

A small bunch of parsley

Serves 4-6

CUT THE ONION into small, pea-sized dice. Finely chop the leek, putting the green parts aside for later. Cut the celery, carrot, courgette and green beans into small, diagonal pieces. Warm some oil in a pan and add the onions and leek whites, plus a pinch of salt. Cook them over a low heat, till soft. Layer the carrot, celery and courgette over the onions and add a ladleful of stock or water. Leave it to simmer gently, for 10-15 minutes.

COOK THE PEAS, chopped leek greens and green beans in a pan of boiling, salted water. When they are tender but still bright green, lift them out with a slotted spoon and spread them over a plate to cool. Pour the stock into the pan with the onions and other vegetables and bring it to a gentle simmer. Stir in the peas, beans and leek greens. Ladle the soup into bowls and sprinkle it with some finely chopped parsley.

33

Soup au pistou

A broth of vegetables and white beans, this is traditionally garnished with a pistou, made from garlic and herbs crushed with oil. You can leave out the garnish, but it is well worth it on occasion, as it adds an intense shot of flavour to the soup.

GF, V, DF

1 onion

1 leek

2 carrots

¼ of a medium-sized squash *(butternut, hokkaido)*

2 stems of celery

A few chestnut mushrooms

A handful of green beans

100g / 3 ½ oz dried haricot or butter beans

   (or one tin of cooked beans)

1 litre / 2 pints of vegetable stock

Crushed basil pistou *(see recipe, p. 48)*, to garnish

Serves 4-6

If you are using dried beans, soak them overnight in cold water. Drain them and put them into a pan with plenty of fresh water. Bring them to the boil and cook them for about 35-45 minutes, till tender. Peel and cut the onion into small, 'bean-sized' pieces. Finely slice the leek, putting the green parts aside for later. Slice the mushrooms thinly, halving them first, if they are large. Cut the celery, carrot and green beans into small, diagonal pieces.

34

WARM SOME OIL in a pan and add the onions and leek whites, plus a pinch of salt. Cook them over a low heat, till soft. Layer the mushrooms over the onions and let them cook for a few minutes. Add the carrot, celery and squash, as well as a ladleful of water or stock. Leave it to simmer for 10-15 minutes. Cook the green beans and chopped leek greens in a pan of boiling, salted water. When they are tender, but still bright green, lift them out with a slotted spoon and spread them over a plate, to cool.

Pour the stock into the pan with the onions and other vegetables. Add the cooked, drained white beans and bring the soup back to a gentle simmer. Just before serving, stir in the cooked leeks and green beans. Ladle the soup into shallow bowls and spoon a little basil pistou into each one.

BASIL

35

Pea and watercress soup with mint

This moss green soup is like a tonic, fresh and peppery and full of goodness. If you prefer, make it with spinach or chard, instead of watercress.

GF, V, DF

1 onion

1 leek

2-3 cloves garlic

100g / 3 ½ oz peas *(fresh or frozen)*

1-2 medium-sized potatoes

A large bunch of watercress

A few mint leaves

1 litre / 2 pints of vegetable stock *(or water)*

Serves 4-6

SLICE THE ONION and leeks, putting the leek greens aside for later. Wash the watercress and break off the thick stems. Crush the garlic with a pinch of salt and cut the potato into large, chunky pieces. Warm some oil in a pan and add the onions, garlic and leek whites. Sprinkle them with a pinch of salt and cook them over a low heat, till soft. Layer the potatoes over the onions, adding just enough stock to cover them. Cook them for 20 minutes or so, till tender.

COOK THE PEAS, leek greens and the stems of the watercress in a pan of boiling, salted water. When they are tender but still bright green, lift them out with a slotted spoon and spread them over a plate to cool. Pour the stock (or water) into the pan with the onions and potato. Bring it up to a gentle simmer and then stir in the cooked greens, the watercress leaves and the mint. Blend it smooth with a hand blender, seasoning it with more salt, if needed.

Onion soup with mushrooms and thyme

The trick with good onion soup is to cook the onions slowly – let them stew in their own juices, till so sticky and tender, they almost melt.

GF, V, DF

4-5 onions

2-3 cloves of garlic

A few chestnut mushrooms

1-2 tsp miso

2 tbsp tamari *(or soy sauce)*

A few sprigs of fresh thyme *(or ½ tsp dried herbs)*

1 ½ litres / 3 pints of vegetable stock

A small bunch of parsley *(optional)*

Serves 4-6

Cut the onions into thin, half moon slices and crush the garlic with a pinch of salt. Cut the mushrooms into slices, halving them first, if they are large. Finely chop the thyme and the parsley. Warm some oil in a pan and add the onion and garlic, plus a pinch of salt. Cook them over a very low heat for 20-30 minutes, till buttery soft.

Layer the mushrooms over the onions and let them steam for a few minutes. Add the stock and the thyme and leave the soup to simmer. Just before serving, stir in the miso and tamari (or soy sauce). Ladle the soup into bowls and sprinkle it with finely chopped parsley.

TAMARI BROTH WITH BROCCOLI AND UDON NOODLES

Udon noodles are Japanese semi-wholewheat noodles, which have a pale, nutty brown colour, when cooked. If they are not available, use rice noodles instead.

V, DF

1 x 250g packet of Udon noodles

1-2 onions

1-2 cloves of garlic

A thumbnail-sized piece of ginger

A few shitake mushrooms *(optional)*

A small head of broccoli

1 litre / 2 pints of vegetable stock

2 tbsp tamari *(or soy sauce)*

1-2 tbsp mirin *(optional)*

A couple of spring onions, to garnish *(optional)*

Serves 4-6

COOK THE UDON NOODLES in a large pan of simmering water for 8-10 minutes. Drain them, rinse them under cold running water and then set them aside. Cut the broccoli into small florets. Cook them in a pan of boiling, salted water. When they are tender but still bright green, lift them out with a slotted spoon and spread them over a plate to cool.

CUT THE ONIONS into thin, half moon slices and finely chop the garlic. Cut the mushrooms into thin slices, halving them first if they are large. Grate the ginger and cut the spring onions finely, on the diagonal.

38

Warm some sesame (or sunflower) oil in a pan and add the onions and garlic, plus a pinch of salt. Cook them slowly over a low heat, till soft. Layer the mushrooms over the onions and let them steam for a few minutes. Add the stock and bring the soup up to a gentle simmer.

Just before serving, stir in the Udon noodles, the cooked broccoli and the juice pressed from the grated ginger. Season the soup with the mirin and then tamari (or soy sauce). Ladle it into bowls and sprinkle it with finely sliced spring onions.

Chunky vegetable soup with miso

Look out for salsify or burdock on market stalls and in small green-grocers. Related to the daisy, these mild-flavoured root vegetables are full of goodness and have cleansing properties. They look like nothing special until they are peeled, when the bright white core is revealed. If neither salsify nor burdock are available, leave them out, or swap them for something like parsnip, turnip or celeriac.

GF, V, DF

1 onion

2 stems of celery

2 carrots

1 salsify or burdock root *(if available)*

Half a small swede *(optional)*

¼ of a medium-sized squash *(butternut, hokkaido)*

A thumbnail-sized piece of ginger *(optional)*

4-5 pieces of dried mushroom

    (shitake, porcini, or mixed wild mushrooms)

1 litre / 2 pints of vegetable stock

1-2 tsp miso paste

Serves 4-6

Soak the dried mushrooms in a cup of boiling water, for about 20 minutes. When they are soft enough, cut them into fine slices. Cut the onion, carrots, celery, swede, squash and salsify or burdock (if using) into chunky, thumbnail-sized pieces.

40

Warm some oil in a large pan and add the onions, plus a pinch of salt. Cook them slowly over a low heat, till soft. Layer the carrots, celery, swede, squash and salsify or burdock over the onions, adding a ladleful of water or stock. Place a small lid (or a piece of baking parchment), inside the saucepan and directly on top of the vegetables. Cook the vegetables over a low heat for 20 minutes or so, till tender. Remove the lid (or baking parchment) and pour in the rest of the stock, as well as the sliced mushrooms and the liquid from soaking them. Bring the soup back to a gentle simmer and just before serving it, stir in the miso and the juice pressed from the grated ginger.

Tip: Authentic miso soup is usually garnished with finely sliced scallions (or spring onions) and gomasio, a seasoning made of toasted sesame seeds crushed with salt.

41

CREAMY SWEET POTATO SOUP
WITH COCONUT

Mild and sweet, this soup is popular with children. For added texture, we sometimes serve it sprinkled with a little toasted, desiccated coconut.

GF, V, DF

1-2 onions

1 medium leek *(white part only)*

2 carrots

2 stems of celery

3-4 cloves of garlic

2 medium-sized sweet potatoes

1 litre / 2 pints of vegetable stock *(or water)*

1-2 tbsp coconut cream

A thumbnail-sized piece of ginger *(optional)*

Serves 4-6

SLICE THE ONIONS, leeks and celery and crush the garlic. Peel and roughly chop the carrots and sweet potatoes. Warm some oil in a pan and add the onion and leek, plus a pinch of salt. Cook them slowly over a low heat, till soft.

Layer the carrot, celery and sweet potato over the onions and add a ladleful of water or stock. Place a small lid (or a piece of baking parchment), inside the saucepan and directly on top of the vegetables.

Cook the vegetables over a low heat for 10-15 minutes or so. Remove the lid (or baking parchment) and pour in the rest of the stock (or water). Add the coconut cream and the juice pressed from the grated ginger. Blend the soup with a hand blender, adding more stock or water, if needed, so as to get a creamy, fluid consistency.

Variation: Swap the sweet potato for butternut squash, or hokkaido, or another variety of squash.

PUY LENTIL AND VEGETABLE SOUP

Dark and savoury, this is a true winter warmer.

GF, V, DF

1 onion

1 leek *(white part only)*

2 carrots

2 stems of celery

¼ of a medium-sized squash *(butternut, hokkaido)*

A few chestnut mushrooms

100g / 3 ½ oz puy lentils

1 litre / 2 pints of vegetable stock *(or water)*

2 tbsp tamari *(or soy sauce)*

1 tbsp tomato puree

Serves 4-6

PUT THE PUY LENTILS into a pan with plenty of water and perhaps a bay leaf and bring it to the boil. Leave it to simmer for 30-35 minutes, till the lentils are tender. Cut the onion, leeks, celery, carrot and squash, into small dice – as close to 'lentil-size' as possible. Finely slice the mushrooms, cutting them in half if they are large.

WARM SOME OIL in a pan and add the onions and leek whites, plus a pinch of salt. Cook them slowly over a low heat, till soft. Layer the mushrooms over the onions and let them cook for a few minutes. Add the carrot, celery and squash, as well as a ladleful of stock or water. Place a small lid (or a piece of baking parchment), inside the saucepan and directly on top of the vegetables. Cook the vegetables over a low heat for 10-15 minutes or so. Remove the lid (or baking parchment) and pour in the rest of the stock (or water). Stir in the drained, cooked puy lentils and the tomato puree. Ladle half a litre / one pint of the soup into a measuring jug and blend it smooth with a hand blender. Return it to the pan and bring the soup back to a gentle simmer. Season it with tamari (or soy sauce).

BAY LEAF

Leek and potato soup
with white miso

White miso gives sweetness and depth of flavour to this winter classic, but it is by no mean essential and can easily be left out, if preferred.

GF, V, DF

  1 onion
  3-4 leeks
  3-4 medium-sized potatoes *(a floury type)*
  1-2 tsp white miso *(optional)*
  1 litre / 2 pints of vegetable stock *(or water)*

Serves 4-6

Slice the leek into thin rounds, putting aside the green parts for later. Finely slice the onion. Peel the potatoes and cut them into thumbnail-sized pieces. Warm some oil in a pan and add the onion and leek. Sprinkle them with a pinch of salt and cook them slowly over a low heat, till soft and translucent. Layer the potato over the onion and leeks and add just enough water or stock to cover them. Leave them to cook over a low heat for 20 minutes or so.

Finely slice the leek greens. Cook them in a pan of boiling, salted water. When they are tender but still bright green, lift them out with a slotted spoon and spread them over a plate to cool. Ladle half a litre / one pint of the soup into a measuring jug and blend it smooth with a hand blender. Return it to the pan and bring it back to a gentle simmer. Just before serving, stir in the white miso and the cooked leek greens.

ADUKI BEAN AND CARROT SOUP

Aduki beans are small, oval-shaped red beans, that look pretty paired with carrot, in this warming, earthy soup.

GF, V, DF

3-4 onions

1-2 cloves of garlic

4-5 carrots

2 stems of celery *(optional)*

Half a small bulb of fennel *(optional)*

100g/3 ½ oz dried aduki beans *(or one tin of cooked beans)*

1 litre / 2 pints of vegetable stock

1-2 tbsp tamari *(or soy sauce)*

Serves 4-6

IF YOU ARE using dried aduki beans, soak them overnight in cold water. Drain them and put them into a pan with plenty of fresh water. Bring them to the boil and cook them for about 35 minutes, till tender. Cut the onions, celery, carrot and fennel into roughly 'bean-sized' pieces and finely chop the garlic.

WARM SOME OIL in a pan and add the onions and garlic, plus a pinch of salt. Cook them over a low heat, till soft. Add the celery, carrot and fennel, along with a ladleful of stock or water. Place a small lid (or a piece of baking parchment), inside the saucepan and directly on top of the vegetables. Cook the vegetables over a low heat for 10-15 minutes or so. Remove the lid (or baking parchment) and pour in the rest of the stock. Stir in the drained, cooked aduki beans. Ladle about a quarter of the soup into a measuring jug and blend it smooth with a hand blender. Return it to the pan and bring it back to a gentle simmer. Season the soup with tamari (or soy sauce).

Crushed basil pistou

Serve this trickled over a simple bean and vegetable soup, for a classic, summery soup au pistou (see recipe, p. 34).

GF, V, DF

- A handful of basil
- 1-2 cloves of garlic
- 5-6 tbsp extra virgin olive oil

Peel and crush the garlic with a pinch of salt and finely chop the basil. Blend it with the garlic, oil and lemon juice, using a mortar and pestle. Add more oil if it seems too thick – it should be somewhere between a dressing and a pesto in consistency. To serve, ladle soup into individual bowls and spoon a little of the crushed basil pistou into each one.

Crushed chili pistou

Use this to give a fiery kick to a wintry soup, like aduki bean and carrot, or puy lentil and vegetable soup.

GF, V, DF

- 1 small red chili
- 5-6 tbsp oil

Slice the chili in half and take out the seeds. Chop it up finely. Crush the chopped chili with a pinch of salt and the oil, using a pestle and mortar. Add more oil, if it needs loosening. To serve, ladle the soup into bowls and trickle a little of the crushed chili over the top.

THE SALAD BOWL

THE SALAD BOWL

A SALAD NEEDN'T BE an afterthought. It can be a meal in itself, full of different textures and flavours. Salads are at their best when there is plenty of contrast – between crunchy raw salad leaves and softer, cooked vegetables, or between sharp dressings and the gentle flavour of a grain. Even the simplest of leafy green salads can be transformed just by adding a little alfalfa, some toasted seeds, chopped herbs and a mustard vinaigrette. The Star Anise salad, a lunchtime staple at the café, is usually a combination of mixed leaves, with grilled or wokked vegetables, maybe some blanched green beans, some pickled beetroot or radish and something hot and crispy, like a mini rissole.

When choosing salad leaves, it helps to avoid the ubiquitous iceberg, cos and butterhead lettuces and instead look out for the frilly varieties like oakleaf and rocket. These generally have more crispness, colour and flavour to them. In macrobiotic cooking, raw foods are felt to be less digestible than cooked foods, so although we use raw salad leaves, we also use a lot of cooked vegetables in our salads. Cooking vegetables need not necessarily mean blanching, frying or roasting – salting and pickling are also forms of 'cooking', that enable food to be more easily digested.

For a salad of grain or pasta, try to add a mixture of vegetables cooked in different ways, as well as chopped herbs and something like a lemon dressing. A well-kept secret of making this kind of salad is that you need to add a small amount of something with a very intense flavour. Black olives, sun-dried tomatoes, capers and anchovies are all strongly flavoured and help to punctuate a salad. Set against this, you have the cleaner flavours of things like lightly blanched carrots, green beans and courgette. Salads of beans, lentils or grains are also best dressed while still warm, as the flavour of the dressing is absorbed more readily. Don't be mean with the salt and vinegar or lemon juice, as these earthy salads need some sharpening up, or else they can suffer from blandness.

To make all the different ingredients 'sit' well together in a salad, think about the size and shape of the 'cut', when preparing vegetables. A pasta salad of fusilli or penne works well when the other vegetables are cut into long, thin pieces of roughly the same size as the pasta. In grain salads, let the size of 'cut' be guided by the largest bean or grain used in the salad – vegetables can be cut into 'bean-size' dice in some salads and into very fine, 'grain-size' dice in others.

LEAFY GREEN SALAD WITH SPRINKLES

GF, V, DF

1 small head of lettuce *(a frilly type, like oakleaf)*

A handful of salad leaves *(spinach, rocket, radicchio)*

4 tbsp sprouting seeds *(alfalfa, radish seeds)*

Some seasoned toasted seeds (see recipe, p. 63)

For the vinaigrette:

5-6 tbsp extra virgin olive oil

1-2 tbsp balsamic vinegar *(or red/white wine vinegar)*

1-2 tbsp lemon juice *(optional)*

Serves 4-6

WASH THE SALAD leaves and dry them using a salad spinner (or parcel them up in a clean, dry tea towel and give it a good shake). Rinse the sprouting seeds in a sieve and leave them to drain.

TO MAKE THE VINAIGRETTE, mix the oil, vinegar, lemon juice and a pinch of salt in the bottom of a large salad bowl. Pile the salad leaves into the bowl and gently fold them over and over, so that they are lightly coated. Add the sprouting seeds and scatter the toasted seeds over the top.

STAR ANISE SALAD

Crispy salad leaves, green beans, juicy grilled vegetables and perhaps some tart pickled beetroot, on the side.

GF, V, DF

  1 small head of lettuce *(a frilly type, like oakleaf)*

  A handful of green beans

  2 red peppers

  1 medium-sized courgette

  1-2 tbsp olive oil

  3-4 tbsp pickled beetroot (see recipe, p. 71)

For the grain mustard vinaigrette:

  1 tsp wholegrain mustard

  1 tbsp white wine or cider vinegar

  1-2 tbsp lemon juice *(optional)*

  1 tsp apple juice concentrate *(or ½ tsp honey)*

  3-4 tbsp olive oil

Serves 4-6

CUT THE PEPPERS and the courgette into large, chunky slices or strips and place them on a baking tray. Add the oil and a pinch of salt and toss the vegetables, so that they are evenly coated. Grill them on a medium to high heat, for 10-15 minutes. When cooked, the vegetables will be soft and juicy and slightly scorched at the edges.

54

Cut the green beans in half if they are long and remove the tips. Cook them in a pan of boiling, salted water. When they are tender, but still bright green, lift them out with a slotted spoon and spread them over a plate, to cool.

Wash the salad leaves and dry them using a salad spinner (or parcel them up in a clean, dry tea towel and give it a good shake). In the bottom of a large salad bowl, mix together the mustard, vinegar, lemon juice, apple concentrate and oil and a pinch of salt, to make the vinaigrette. Toss the salad leaves in the vinaigrette, coating them evenly. Serve the salad with the grilled vegetables and green beans and a spoonful of beetroot relish.

Herby quinoa and millet tabbouleh

Quinoa and millet, cooked together, make a light and fluffy grain, which works well in this delicate, gluten-free salad. If preferred, just quinoa can be used, or it can be swapped altogether for cracked wheat (the traditional grain used for tabbouleh) or couscous.

GF, V, DF

100g / 3 ½ oz quinoa
100g / 3 ½ oz millet
1 onion
1 carrot
Half a courgette
A few sun-dried tomatoes
A few black olives *(optional)*
A small bunch of parsley
A few leaves of fresh basil *(optional)*
Half a lemon, juice
2-3 tbsp olive oil

Serves 4-6

Put the quinoa and millet into a pan and add 1½ times as much water as grain, plus a pinch of salt. Cook the grain over a high heat for a couple of minutes, then turn it right down and let it simmer for a further 10-15 minutes. Turn off the heat and leave the grain, covered with a lid, to finish cooking in its own steam. After 20 minutes or so, fork through it, so as to loosen it.

CUT THE onion as finely as possible – the smaller, the better. Do the same with the carrot and courgette. Finely chop the herbs and cut the sun-dried tomatoes and olives into thin slivers (removing the olive stones, if they have them).

WARM SOME oil in a pan and cook the onion with a pinch of salt, till soft. Layer the chopped carrot and courgette over the onions and let them cook for 5-10 minutes.

TIP THE GRAIN into a large bowl and add the cooked onion, carrot, courgette, olives, sun-dried tomatoes and chopped herbs. Gently fold in the lemon juice and olive oil and season it with salt (dissolved in a little hot water), or tamari. Serve it with a simple green salad, for a light meal, or as part of a spread, with a couple of other salads.

RICE WITH GREEN LENTILS, OLIVES AND HERBS

This salad works because of the different shades of green set against the creamy colour of the rice. Add some crumbled feta, goats cheese, or basil tofu as a highlight, if you like.

GF, V, DF

100g / 3 ½ oz green lentils *(or puy lentils)*
250g / 9 oz long-grain *(or short-grain)* brown rice
1 onion
100g / 3 ½ oz green olives
A small bunch of parsley
A small bunch of chives *(optional)*
1 lemon, juice *(and a little zest – optional)*
3-4 tbsp olive oil

Serves 4-6

PUT THE RICE into a pan and add twice as much water as grain, plus a pinch of salt. Cook the rice over a medium heat, till all the water has been absorbed. Put the lentils into another pan and cover them with plenty of water. Let them simmer for about 40 minutes, till tender. Leave the lentils to cool in their cooking liquid and then drain them and rinse them in cold water.

CUT THE ONION into small, 'lentil-sized' pieces. Warm some oil in a pan and cook the onion with a pinch of salt, till soft. Finely chop the herbs and cut the green olives into thin slivers (removing the stones, if they have them). Tip the cooked rice into a large bowl. Add the drained lentils, cooked onion, olives and chopped herbs. Fold in the lemon juice, lemon zest and olive oil and season it with salt (dissolved in a little hot water) or tamari. Serve it with a simple green salad, for a light lunch, or as part of a spread, with a couple of other salads.

Tip: Use a pressure cooker (if you dare) for cooking the lentils, as they hold their shape better when cooked this way. This salad works best if the rice and lentils have been cooked the previous day.

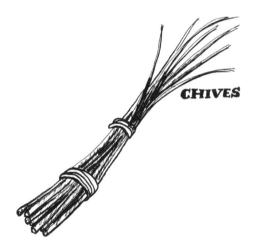

CHIVES

Penne salad with crunchy vegetable spears

British asparagus is available for a month or two in the spring. Cut into lengths and lightly blanched, it turns this simple pasta salad into something out of the ordinary.

V, DF

300g / 11 oz penne
   (or another tube-shaped pasta)
4-5 tbsp olive oil
A small bunch of asparagus *(if available)*
2-3 carrots
1 small courgette
A handful of green beans *(optional)*
1 red onion
Half a lemon, juice
A small bunch of parsley

Serves 4-6

Cook the pasta in a large pan of boiling, salted water. Drain it and stir in a tablespoon or two of olive oil. Cut the onion into large dice and finely chop the parsley. Snap off the bottom of the asparagus spears and peel them, if they seem tough. Cut the spears into short strips, about the same length as the cooked pasta. Cut the green beans, courgette and carrot into similar-sized strips.

WARM SOME OIL in a pan and cook the onion, till soft. Add the carrot and let it simmer for 10-15 minutes. Cook green beans, courgette and asparagus in a pan of boiling, salted water. When they are tender but still bright green, lift them out with a slotted spoon and spread them over a plate to cool.

TIP THE PASTA into a large bowl and add the onion, carrot and celery, as well as the cooked green beans and asparagus. Season it with salt (dissolved in a little hot water) and fold in the chopped parsley, lemon juice and more olive oil. Serve it with some rocket, or torn basil leaves, or just as it is.

TANGLED CARROT RIBBON SALAD

So called, because a peeler is used to create long, thin ribbons. We like to braise the carrot ribbons in the oven, to make them more tender, but they are equally good raw.

GF, V, DF

5-6 carrots

2-3 tbsp sesame seeds

Half a lemon, juice

2 tbsp rice vinegar *(or white wine vinegar)*

2 tbsp sesame oil *(or sunflower oil)*

Serves 4-6

TOAST THE SESAME SEEDS in a small frying pan, over a low heat, till they start to colour. Tip them into a bowl and set them aside. Peel the carrots and cut them in half lengthways, if they are very broad. Using a peeler, peel down the whole length of the carrot, to make ribbons. Line a baking tray with baking parchment and evenly distribute the carrot ribbons over it. Cover them with another sheet of baking parchment. Braise them in the oven for 10-15 minutes, at 150°C (Fan 130°C) / Gas mark 5, till they start to look translucent, but are still quite crunchy.

IN A LARGE BOWL, stir together the vinegar, lemon juice, sesame oil and a pinch of salt, to make the dressing. Toss the carrot ribbons in the dressing and sprinkle them with the toasted sesame seeds.

TIP: If you like the flavour of aniseed, try using fennel or caraway seeds instead of sesame seeds. Toast them in the same way. Fennel and caraway have traditionally been used in cooking for aiding good digestion.

SEASONED TOASTED SEEDS

Vary the seeds according to what you like. Use just one kind, or a mixture of different ones. Sprinkle them over salads or main dishes, or just snack on them, as they are.

GF, V, DF

A handful each of sunflower seeds, pumpkin seeds
   and sesame seeds
1-2 tbsp golden linseeds *(optional)*
2 tbsp tamari *(or soy sauce)*
1-2 tsp rice syrup *(or agave syrup)*

RINSE THE SEEDS, by putting them into a sieve and running them under cold water (this allows them to swell slightly and so remain tender). Spread them out on a baking tray and put them in the oven for 20-25 minutes, at 150°C (Fan 130°C) / Gas mark 5. Take them out and spoon over the tamari (or soy sauce) and the syrup. Stir the seeds, so as to coat them evenly. Return the tray to the oven for another five minutes, to dry them out a little more. Once cool, fork through the seeds, to break up any clusters.

RED AND GREEN BEAN SALAD

GF, V, DF

200g / 7 oz dried kidney beans *(or 2 tins of cooked beans)*
2 red onions
1 clove of garlic
A large handful of green beans
4-6 tbsp olive oil
3-4 tbsp red wine vinegar
1 tbsp rice syrup *(or agave syrup) (optional)*
½ tsp umiboshi paste *(optional)*
A pinch of cayenne pepper *(optional)*
A small bunch of fresh coriander

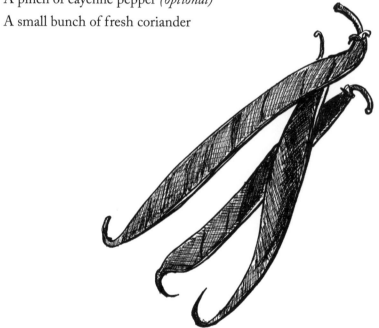

Serves 4-6

IF YOU ARE using dried beans, soak them overnight in cold water. Drain them and put them into a pan with plenty of fresh water. Bring them to the boil and cook them for about 45 minutes, till tender. Leave them to cool in their cooking liquid and then drain them and rinse them in cold water.

FINELY CHOP the onion and crush the garlic with a pinch of salt. Warm some oil in a small pan and cook the onion and garlic, till soft. Cut the green beans into short lengths. Cook green beans in a pan of boiling, salted water. When they are tender but still bright green, lift them out with a slotted spoon and spread them over a plate to cool.

IN A LARGE BOWL, mix the vinegar, rice syrup, umiboshi and oil with a pinch of cayenne pepper. Add the red kidney beans, cooked green beans, onion and chopped fresh coriander and gently fold them into the dressing. Serve it with a simple green salad, for a light meal, or as part of a spread, with a couple of other salads.

VARIATION: Instead of kidney beans, use cooked puy lentils. Cut the onions and green beans more finely to suit the smaller size of the lentils and dress the salad with balsamic vinegar, lemon juice, olive oil and chopped fresh thyme.

Potato salad with cornichons and rosemary

The chopped rosemary in this picnic classic gives it an earthy, Mediterranean feel. Adding roasted shallots is well worth the extra effort, but if you prefer, leave them out, or swap them for finely chopped chives.

GF, V, DF

1kg / 2 lb potatoes *(small new potatoes, if available)*

4-5 shallots

One small jar of cornichons

4-5 tbsp white wine vinegar *(or cider vinegar)*

6-8 tbsp olive oil

A sprig or two of rosemary

A handful of parsley

Serves 4-6

Roast the shallots by laying them on a baking tray, as they are, with the skins still on. Put them into the oven for 20-30 minutes, at 150°C (Fan 130°C) / Gas mark 5 (this can be done anytime beforehand, when you happen to have the oven on – roasted shallots, onions or garlic keep well, for several days). When cool enough to handle, cut the base and tops off the shallots and slip them out of their skins.

SCRUB THE POTATOES and put them into a large pan with plenty of salted water. Cook them over a medium heat till tender. Drain them and leave them to cool slightly. Cut the potatoes into chunky (but manageable) pieces, or leave them whole, if they are small. Slice the cornichons and roughly chop the roasted shallots. Put the potatoes into a large bowl with the shallots and cornichons. Add the oil, vinegar and a good pinch of salt (dissolved in hot water) and gently fold in the chopped rosemary and parsley.

VARIATION: If you prefer a creamier dressing for potato salad, but don't want to resort to mayonnaise or dairy products, swap the vinaigrette for a lemon and tahini dressing (see recipe, p. 69).

GRAIN MUSTARD VINAIGRETTE

An everyday basic at the café, we make up large quantities of this dressing. It helps to add a small amount of something sweet to balance out the peppery mustard – apple concentrate works beautifully, but if you prefer, honey or rice syrup could be used instead.

GF, V, DF

1 tbsp wholegrain mustard
3-4 tbsp white wine vinegar *(or cider vinegar)*
Half a lemon, juice *(optional)*
1 tbsp apple concentrate *(or ½ tsp honey)*
10-12 tbsp olive oil

IN A BOWL, stir the mustard with the vinegar, lemon juice and apple concentrate. Add the oil and blend it in with a whisk, till you have a fluid, smooth consistency. Season it with salt or tamari.

LEMON AND TAHINI DRESSING

This is a richer, creamier dressing than the mustard vinaigrette, that works well in place of mayonnaise.

GF, V, DF

1 lemon, juice
2-3 tbsp tahini
4-5 tbsp of boiling water
½ tsp umiboshi paste *(optional)*
6-8 tbsp olive oil

PUT THE LEMON JUICE, tahini and umiboshi paste (if using) into a bowl and add the boiling water. Blend them together with a whisk, till you have a smooth, creamy consistency (alternatively, use a blender). Season the dressing with salt or tamari.

Pickled radish slices

Ume plum seasoning is branded as a Japanese vinegar-alternative. Sour, but also salty, it is the colour of rosé wine. Marinating radish slices in it makes them tender and also turns them a vivid pink colour.

GF, V, DF

150g / 5 oz radishes *(about 12 small radishes)*

50ml / 2 fl oz Ume plum seasoning

2-3 tbsp rice vinegar *(or white wine vinegar)*

Makes about 150g / 5 oz

Cut the radishes into quarters and slice them paper-thin. Put the Ume plum seasoning and vinegar into a small pan with 2-3 tbsp water and bring it to the boil. Take it off the heat and stir in the radish slices. Leave them to marinate for 10-15 minutes. Drain off the excess seasoning (this can be kept and used again, for seasoning other dishes). The pickled radish slices can be served straightaway, or stored in a jar, in the fridge. Use them in sandwiches and salads, or alongside a main dish.

PICKLED BEETROOT

Add this to salads, or serve it alongside a main dish – wherever there is a shortage of something crunchy, tart and purple.

GF, V, DF

3-4 medium-sized beetroot

3-4 tbsp balsamic vinegar

1 tsp ground cumin

Makes about 300g / 11 oz

WASH THE BEETROOT and cut away the tops and roots. Cook them in a pan of boiling water for 20-30 minutes, till tender, though still quite firm to the touch. Drain the beetroot and when cool enough to handle, slip them out of their skins. Cut them into pea-sized dice.

HEAT SOME OIL in a small pan and add the ground cumin. Let the spice froth for a few seconds and then add the balsamic vinegar. Turn off the heat and pour the spiced vinegar over the beetroot. Stir it in and season it with salt.

72

QUICK STOVE TOP SUPPERS

QUICK STOVE-TOP SUPPERS

JUST BECAUSE a meal needs to be ready in under an hour, doesn't mean it can't be pulled together from fresh, basic ingredients. So often, the temptation is to reach for the jar of ready-made sauce, rummage around in the freezer for some protein and serve up a meal based on convenience foods. It takes more time and mental effort to prepare food from scratch - tomato sauce made with fresh tomatoes feels so much more challenging than opening a tin.

There is no denying that convenience food is incredibly useful and can save time, but ideally it should play second fiddle to fresh, basic ingredients. By all means, simplify a dish if it makes things easier – pare it down to just a few good quality ingredients, cooked and seasoned with care. Be generous with fresh vegetables, grains, nuts, seeds, pulses and fruit and be sparing with the tins, packets and jars and the food will ultimately be more nourishing and vibrant.

Pasta is the fallback staple for many of us, when it comes to preparing meals in a hurry. As a rule, it goes down well with adults and children alike and makes for a quick, fuss-free meal. For those with wheat or gluten intolerance, there are corn, rice and spelt versions, among others, to choose from. At the café, we tend to serve pasta with a fresh tomato sauce, a herby pesto, or creamy sauces made with dairy-free alternatives. Other quick dishes that we like to rustle up from time to time include risottos, savoury grain dishes and stir-fried vegetables with noodles.

PASTA WITH POOR MAN'S PESTO

Our pesto is dairy-free, unlike most shop-bought pesto and is quick and simple to make, if you have a blender. Toasted cashew nuts work well instead of pine nuts, (which are usually used for pesto) and cost a lot less. We tend to use rocket, but it can be swapped for spinach, or other leafy greens.

V, DF

500g / 1 lb pasta
  (penne, fusilli, or another shape)
For the pesto:
  50g / 1 ½ oz rocket *(a large handful)*
  A small bunch of fresh basil
  50g / 2 oz cashew nuts
  1-2 cloves of garlic
  1-2 tbsp lemon juice
  75g / 3 oz extra virgin olive oil

Serves 4-6

TOAST THE CASHEW NUTS by putting them in a large frying pan and 'dry-roasting' them. Keep the heat very low and stir them often, so that they colour evenly. Let them cool and then tip them into a blender. Crush the garlic with a pinch of salt and add it to the toasted cashew nuts.

WASH THE ROCKET and basil and chop it up roughly. Add it to the cashew nuts and garlic, along with the olive oil and lemon juice. Blend it coarsely, seasoning it with more salt, or adding some more olive oil, if it needs loosening up.

Cook the pasta in a large pan of salted, boiling water. Stir in the pesto and serve it as it is, or with some grated cheese and a leafy green salad.

Variations: Add other vegetables to the pasta and pesto, like strips of grilled or sautéed courgette or mushroom, cooked spinach, or asparagus spears, if available.

PARSLEY

PASTA WITH CREAMY MUSHROOM AND SPINACH SAUCE

Classic béchamel sauce is made with milk and butter, but using soya milk and olive oil, you can make a lighter, dairy-free version, which is still very silky and creamy.

Can be V, DF

500g /1 lb pasta
  (penne, shells, or another shape)
150g / 5 oz chestnut mushrooms
100g / 3 ½ oz spinach
For the béchamel sauce:
350ml / 12 fl oz milk *(or soya milk)*
2-3 tbsp olive oil
50g / 2 oz plain flour *(or white spelt flour)*
1 small clove of garlic *(optional)*

Serves 4-6

ROUGHLY CHOP THE SPINACH and finely slice the mushrooms. Warm some oil in a pan and cook the mushrooms for a few minutes, till tender. Put the spinach in another pan, with a small amount of water. Cook it very briefly over a high heat and then drain it and spread it over a plate, to cool.

To MAKE THE BÉCHAMEL sauce, finely chop the garlic. Warm the oil in a pan and add the garlic. Cook it till it starts to colour and then add the flour. Pour in a portion of the milk (or soya milk) and stir it with a whisk, till it starts to thicken.

ADD THE REST of the milk, bit by bit, stirring the sauce frequently. Season it with a pinch of salt and let it simmer for a few minutes. Take it off the heat and set it aside. Cook the pasta in a pan of boiling, salted water. Drain it and stir in a couple of tablespoons of olive oil. Fold in the béchamel sauce, as well as the mushrooms and spinach.

TIP: If you want to pull out all the stops, infuse the milk (or soya milk) for the béchamel, by letting it simmer for 20-30 minutes with a bay leaf and a quarter of an onion, studded with a couple of cloves. Add 1-2 tbsp of white wine to the béchamel sauce and mix in a few wild mushrooms with the chestnut mushrooms. Garnish the dish with finely chopped parsley and ground black pepper.

Stir-fried vegetables with tofu and Udon noodles

Use whichever vegetables you like in the stir-fry – green beans, fennel and some cabbage varieties (like spring cabbage) work well. Swap the tofu for whole cashew nuts, or toasted sesame seeds, if you prefer.

GF, V, DF

2 x 250g packets of Udon noodles *(or rice noodles)*

1 packet of plain tofu *(or smoked tofu)*

1-2 onions

1 bunch of spring onions

4-5 carrots

1 courgette

2 red peppers

A few chestnut mushrooms

2-3 cloves of garlic

A thumbnail-sized piece of ginger *(optional)*

Tamari *(or soy sauce)*

Mirin *(optional)*

Rice vinegar *(or white wine vinegar)*

Sesame oil *(or sunflower oil)*

Serves 4-6

Cook the Udon noodles in a large pan of simmering water for 8-10 minutes. Drain them, rinse them under cold running water and then set them aside. Cut the tofu into thumbnail-sized pieces and put it in a shallow dish with 1-2 tbsp tamari (or soy sauce), 1-2 tbsp vinegar and 2-3 tbsp of the sesame (or sunflower) oil. Leave it to marinate.

FINELY CHOP the garlic and the ginger. Thinly slice the mushrooms. Cut the onion into half moon slices and cut the carrots, spring onions, courgette and peppers into short, thin strips.

WARM A GENEROUS AMOUNT of sesame (or sunflower) oil in a wok or large frying pan. Add the garlic and ginger. After a minute or so, add the onions and cover the pan, so that the onions soften in their own steam. Add the carrots next, covering the pan again, but keeping the heat high and tossing the vegetables over from time to time (add a ladleful of water if they start to scorch). Next, add the peppers, courgette and mushrooms. Right at the end, when almost all the liquid has disappeared, season it with 1-2 tbsp mirin and 1-2 tbsp tamari (or soy sauce). Set the stir fried vegetables aside in a dish and keep them warm.

HEAT SOME MORE OIL in the wok or frying pan and cook the drained tofu for 5-10 minutes or so, till lightly coloured. Add the cooked Udon noodles and when they are hot, season them with the liquid from marinating the tofu. Serve the noodles and tofu with the stir-fried vegetables.

VARIATION: Instead of noodles, use cooked brown or white rice, adding it to the tofu in the same way and seasoning it with the marinating liquid.

Savoury rice with toasted, flaked almonds

This is a good way of making use of yesterday's cooked rice, as the grains will have dried a little and will be better able to hold their shape. The quantity of rice is not too important, just use what you have got, if it looks enough.

GF, V, DF

300g / 11 oz long grain brown rice
   (or about 800g / 1 ¾ lb cooked rice)
1 onion
1-2 carrots
2 stems of celery
¼ of a medium-sized squash *(butternut, hokkaido)*
Half a courgette *(optional)*
A small bunch of spring onions
50g / 2 oz of flaked almonds
Tamari *(or soy sauce)*

CORIANDER

Serves 4-6

TOAST THE FLAKED ALMONDS, by putting them in a large frying pan and 'dry-roasting' them over a low heat. Stir them from time to time, so that they colour evenly. Put the rice into a pan, with twice as much water as grain, plus a pinch of salt. Cook it over a medium heat, till all the water has been absorbed (for brown rice, this takes about 35 minutes).

CHOP THE ONION very finely – the smaller, the better. Cut the carrots, celery, squash and courgette into tiny dice and finely slice the spring onions. Warm some oil in a pan and cook the onion with a pinch of salt, till it turns translucent. Layer the carrot, celery and squash over the onions and add a ladleful of water. Cook them over a low heat for 5-10 minutes or so, till they start to soften. Add the courgette and cook it for a few minutes more.

STIR THE cooked rice through the vegetables, along with the finely sliced spring onions and most of the toasted flaked almonds. Gently warm it through and season it with tamari (or soy sauce). Scatter the rest of the toasted flaked almonds over the rice and serve it with sautéed greens, or a leafy salad.

MUSHROOM RISOTTO WITH THYME

GF, V, DF

1 onion *(or shallot)*

2 cloves of garlic

150g / 5 oz chestnut mushrooms

A few dried mushroom pieces

   (shitake, porcini or mixed wild mushrooms)

300g / 11 oz short-grain brown rice

1200ml / 2 ½ pints vegetable stock *(or water)*

A splash of white wine *(optional)*

A small bunch of parsley

Serves 4-6

PUT THE DRIED MUSHROOMS into a cup and cover them with boiling water. Leave them to soak for half an hour or so, till soft enough to cut into thin slivers. Cut the fresh mushrooms into slices and finely chop the onion and garlic.

WARM SOME OIL in a saucepan and add the onion and garlic, plus a pinch of salt. Cook them over a low heat, till soft. Add the mushrooms and the rice and cook the mixture for a few minutes, till the grains start to look translucent. Pour in the wine (if using) and some of the stock and let it simmer, till it is absorbed. Add more stock, a ladleful at a time, stirring the rice from time to time.

LET IT COOK over a low heat for about 20 minutes, till the grains are tender. Add more stock if it needs loosening up a bit; it should be creamy, but at the same time substantial enough to eat with a fork. Stir in the chopped thyme and more salt, if needed. Serve the risotto in shallow soup plates. Spoon a little olive oil over the top and sprinkle it with some finely chopped parsley.

ROASTED SQUASH AND CHESTNUT RISOTTO

BEFORE MAKING the risotto, cut half a squash (butternut, hokkaido) into thumbnail-sized pieces and lay them on a baking tray. Add a little oil and salt and roast them in the oven for 10-15 minutes, at 180°C (Fan 160°C) / Gas Mark 6. Roughly chop up a handful of pre-cooked chestnuts.

PREPARE THE RISOTTO in the same way as before, but instead of the mushrooms, stir in the chestnuts and some of the roasted squash, right at the end. Serve the risotto in shallow soup plates, with more roasted squash pieces piled on top, and, if occasion calls for it, trickle some basil pistou (see recipe, p.48) over it all as well.

SPAGHETTI WITH FRESH TOMATO SAUCE AND BASIL

The longer you cook the tomato sauce the better – as it cooks, the tomatoes lose their natural bitterness. The ideal is a thick, almost 'jammy' sauce, which has become slightly caramelised and sweet.

V, DF

500g / 1 lb spaghetti

For the tomato sauce:

1-2 onions (or shallots)

1-2 stems of celery

1-2 carrots

500g / 1 lb ripe tomatoes *(about 4-5 medium-sized ones)*

A small bunch of fresh basil

Serves 4-6

FINELY CHOP THE ONION, celery and carrot and crush the garlic with a pinch of salt. Warm some oil in a large pan and cook the onion and garlic over a low heat, till soft. Add the carrot and celery and cook them for a few minutes. Chop the tomatoes (peel them first if you prefer, by scoring them with a knife, covering them with boiling water for half a minute and then slipping off their skins). Add the chopped tomato to the vegetables and some more salt. Let the sauce simmer for 20-30 minutes, or longer. Cook the spaghetti in a large pan of boiling, salted water. Drain it and stir in the tomato sauce and fresh basil. Add a few tablespoons of extra virgin olive oil right at the end, to give it a glossy sheen.

TIP: For an extra smooth sauce, blend the chopped tomatoes first, using a hand-blender, before adding them to the sauce.

OVEN
BAKES&ONEPOT
MEALS

OVEN BAKES AND ONE-POT MEALS

THESE ARE THE HOME-MADE EQUIVALENT of ready-meals. They take a small amount of planning and call for some preparation in advance, but once you have made the dish, there is almost no call for further effort on your part. Pulling a meal together is then simply a matter of warming the dish through again and perhaps cooking some greens or throwing together a leafy salad. If you play your cards right and prepare a larger quantity, you might even have the makings of a meal for the following day as well.

Puy lentil and vegetable shepherd's pie

Creamy mash hides a layer of rich, savoury puy lentils and vegetables.

GF, can be V, DF

For the mash:

750g / 1 ½ lb potatoes

1-2 parsnips *(optional)*

1 small swede *(optional)*

2-3 tbsp olive oil

A few tablespoons of milk *(or soya milk)*

Nutmeg *(optional)*

For the filling:

150g / 5 oz puy lentils

2 onions

1-2 leeks *(white part only)*

2-3 stems of celery

3-4 carrots

A few chestnut mushrooms

2 tbsp tomato puree

1 tbsp chopped thyme *(or 1 tsp dried herbs)*

Tamari *(or soy sauce)*

Serves 4-6

PEEL THE POTATOES, swede and parsnips, removing the centre of the parsnips, if they seem tough. Cut them into chunky, similar-sized pieces. Put them into a pan with enough water to cover them and bring them to the boil. Let them simmer for 20-30 minutes, till soft.

Drain them and mash them with the olive oil, milk (or soya milk), some grated nutmeg and a good pinch of salt.

PUT THE PUY LENTILS into a pan with plenty of water and perhaps a bay leaf and bring it to the boil. Leave it to simmer for 30-35 minutes, till the lentils are tender. Cut the onions, celery and carrots into thumbnail-sized pieces and finely slice the leeks and mushrooms.

WARM SOME OIL in a pan and add the onions and leeks, plus a pinch of salt. Cook them over a low heat, till soft. Add the carrots, celery and mushrooms, along with a ladleful of water. Cover the pan with a lid and leave it to simmer. When the carrots are soft, stir in the cooked, drained puy lentils, tomato puree and herbs. Season it with tamari (or soy sauce) and add more water or stock, if needed, to get a loose, moist consistency.

SPOON THE SAVOURY LENTIL mixture into a shallow baking dish and spread the mash over the top. Trickle some olive oil over the mash (this makes it more crispy) and put it into the oven. Bake it at 180°C (Fan 160°C) / Gas Mark 6, for 30-40 minutes.

TIP: For an extra smooth mash, blend the parsnips and swede separately, using a hand blender and then stir them into the mashed potatoes.

Summer vegetable lasagne

This lasagne is less about the red and white sauces and more about the vegetables. The courgette and aubergine are cut into long, broad strips, which are grilled and then layered between the sheets of pasta. A vegetable-rich tomato sauce and a dairy-free béchamel fill in the gaps.

Can be V, DF

250g / 9 oz lasagne sheets

1 medium-sized courgette *(green or yellow)*

1 aubergine

2 onions

2 stems of celery

2 carrots

A few chestnut mushrooms

1 tin of chopped tomatoes

2 tbsp tomato puree

1 tbsp chopped fresh thyme *(or 1 tsp dried herbs)*

For the béchamel sauce:

600ml / 22 fl oz milk *(or soya milk)*

4-5 tbsp olive oil

75g / 3 oz plain flour

Serves 4-6

Cut the courgette and aubergine lengthways into long, thin slices. Lay them on an oven tray and toss them in a little olive oil, so that they are thinly coated. Grill or bake the slices for 20-25 minutes, at 180°C (Fan 160°C) / Gas Mark 6. Cut the onion, celery and carrot into small pieces. Slice the mushrooms and finely chop the garlic.

92

Warm some oil in a pan and add the onion and garlic, plus a pinch of salt. Cook them over a low heat, till soft. Add the carrot, celery and mushrooms and cook them for 10-15 minutes, till tender. Stir in the chopped tomatoes, tomato puree and the fresh thyme and leave the sauce to simmer gently, for 20 minutes or so.

Meanwhile, make the béchamel sauce. Warm the oil in a pan and stir in the flour. Add a portion of the milk (or soya milk) and stir it in with a whisk, till it starts to thicken. Add the rest of the milk, bit by bit, stirring the sauce frequently. Season it with a good pinch of salt and let it simmer for a few minutes. Take it off the heat and set it aside.

Spread some of the tomato and vegetable sauce thinly over the base of a rectangular baking dish. Dip a few sheets of lasagne in cold water and lay them over the filling. Spread some of the béchamel sauce over the lasagne sheets and lay half of the grilled courgette and aubergine slices on top. Cover with more lasagne sheets (dipped in water) and follow with a layer of tomato and vegetable sauce.

Add another layer of béchamel and grilled vegetables, followed by another layer of tomato and vegetable sauce. Finish with a final layer of lasagne sheets and cover them with a thick cloak of béchamel sauce. Trickle some olive oil over the top and add a few thin slices of tomato, if you like. Bake it at 180°C (Fan 160°C) / Gas Mark 6, for 40-45 minutes. Once out of the oven, leave the lasagne to settle for 10 minutes or so, before cutting into it.

Red lentil and vegetable dhal with yellow saffron rice

Pair this with sautéed greens or steamed broccoli, for a warming meal.

GF, V, DF

2 onions

1-2 cloves of garlic

1 small red chili *(optional)*

2-3 stems of celery

2 carrots

½ a medium-sized squash *(butternut, hokkaido)*

200g / 7 oz red split lentils

1 tsp each of ground cumin and coriander

Fresh coriander, to garnish *(optional)*

For the saffron rice:

300g / 11 oz long grain brown rice

A small pinch of saffron filaments

¼ tsp turmeric

Serves 4-6

Put the rice into a pan, with twice the amount of water as grain. Add the saffron and turmeric and a pinch of salt. Cook it over a medium heat, till all the water has been absorbed. Put the red lentils into another pan with plenty of water (and perhaps a bay leaf). Bring them to the boil and leave them to simmer, till tender. Let the rice cool down slightly and then fork through it, to separate the grains.

Cut the onion, carrots, celery and squash into thumbnail-sized pieces. Warm some oil in a pan and add the ground coriander and cumin. Let the spices froth for a few seconds and then add the garlic, chili and onion, plus a pinch of salt. Cook them over a low heat, till the onions become translucent. Layer the celery, carrot and squash over the onions, adding a ladleful of water. Place a small lid (or a piece of baking parchment) inside the saucepan, directly on top of the vegetables. Cook them over a low heat for 10-15 minutes or so, till tender. Remove the lid (or baking parchment) and add the cooked, drained lentils. Warm it through and season it with salt, or tamari (or soy sauce). Spoon the dhal into shallow soup plates, alongside a pile of warm saffron rice and strew it with some fresh coriander.

Sweet potato

and chickpea one-pot

GF, V, DF

Sweet potatoes are quite delicate and it doesn't take long for them to become overcooked and mushy. If you want them to keep their shape, undercook them slightly – they will finish cooking under their own steam.

Serves 4-6

2 onions

1-2 cloves of garlic

2 medium carrots

100g / 3 ½ oz dried chickpeas
   (or one tin of cooked chickpeas)

500g / 1 lb sweet potatoes

A thumbnail-sized piece of ginger

1 tsp each of ground cumin and coriander

1 tbsp arrowroot *(or cornflour)*

Half a lemon, juice

If you are using dried chickpeas, soak them overnight in cold water. Drain them and put them into a pan with plenty of fresh water. Bring it to the boil and cook the chickpeas for about 45 minutes, till tender. Cut the onion, carrots and sweet potato into thumbnail-sized pieces. Finely chop the garlic and grate the ginger.

WARM SOME OIL IN A PAN and add the cumin and coriander. Let the spices froth for a few seconds and then add the onion and garlic, plus a pinch of salt. Cook them over a low heat, till the onions become translucent. Layer the carrots over the onions, adding a ladleful of water. Let them simmer for 5-10 minutes or so, till they start to soften.

ADD THE sweet potatoes and place a small lid (or a piece of baking parchment) inside the saucepan, directly on top of the vegetables. Cook them over a low heat for 5-10 minutes or so, till they are tender, but still have a little crunch to them. Remove the lid (or baking parchment) and add the drained, cooked chickpeas, lemon juice and the juice pressed from the grated ginger.

BRING IT BACK to a gentle simmer. Dissolve the arrowroot in a few tablespoons of cold water and stir it into the vegetables and chickpeas, so that the juices thicken slightly. Serve the stew with cracked wheat, couscous, or rice; or with pieces of warmed pitta bread.

Red kidney bean and vegetable casserole

Pair this with rice or baked potatoes and a leafy green salad. If you prefer it mild rather than spicy, leave out the chili and add some chopped fresh parsley at the end.

GF, V, DF

2 onions

1-2 leeks *(white part only)*

2-3 cloves of garlic

½ small red chili *(optional)*

2-3 stems of celery

4-5 medium carrots

100g / 3 ½ oz dried kidney beans
   (or one tin of cooked beans)

500g / 1 lb fresh tomatoes
   (or one tin of chopped tomatoes)

A few sprigs of fresh thyme *(or 1 tsp dried herbs)*

Serves 4-6

If you are using dried kidney beans, soak them overnight in cold water. Drain them and put them into a pan with plenty of fresh water. Bring them to the boil and cook them for about 45 minutes, till tender. Cut the onion, celery and carrots into thumbnail-sized pieces. Finely chop the garlic and chili and cut the leeks into thin rounds. Chop the tomatoes (peel them first if you prefer, by scoring them with a knife, covering them with boiling water for half a minute and then slipping the skins off).

98

Warm some oil in a pan and add the onion, leek and garlic, plus a pinch of salt. Cook them over a low heat, till soft. Layer the carrots and celery over the onions, adding a ladleful of water. Cook them over a low heat for 10 minutes or so, till tender. Add the chopped tomatoes and a good pinch of salt. Leave the sauce to simmer gently for half an hour (or longer), till it has thickened and darkened in colour slightly. Stir in the drained, cooked kidney beans and the fresh thyme and warm it through.

THYME

99

Spicy black bean chili

Dark and rich, this warming one-pot is thickened by taking out some of the cooked beans and blending them creamy-smooth. Serve the chili with rice, or grilled polenta, or some warm flatbread.

GF, V, DF

2 onions

2-3 stems of celery

Half a small bulb of fennel *(optional)*

2 medium carrots

200g / 3 ½ oz dried black beans – also called 'black turtlebeans'
   (or two tins of beans)

A thumbnail-sized piece of ginger

1 tbsp ground cumin

1 small red chili *(optional)*

Tamari *(or soy sauce)*

Fresh coriander, to garnish *(optional)*

Serves 4-6

If you are using dried black beans, soak them overnight in cold water. Drain them and put them into a pan with plenty of fresh water. Bring them to the boil and cook them for about 35 minutes, till tender. Cut the onion, carrots, celery and fennel into roughly 'black bean-sized' pieces. Finely chop the garlic and chili and grate the ginger.

Warm some oil in a pan and add the cumin. Let it froth for a few seconds and then add the chili, garlic and onion, plus a pinch of salt. Cook them over a low heat, till the onion becomes translucent. Layer the celery, fennel and carrots over the onions and add a ladleful of water. Place a small lid (or a piece of baking parchment) inside the saucepan and directly on top of the vegetables. Cook them over a low heat for 15-20 minutes or so, till tender.

REMOVE the lid (or baking parchment) and add the black beans, including some of their cooking liquid. Ladle half a litre / one pint of the cooked beans and vegetables into a measuring jug and blend them smooth with a hand blender. Return them to the pan and bring the bean chili back to a gentle simmer. Stir in the juice pressed from the grated ginger and season it with tamari (or soy sauce). Serve it with some fresh coriander and perhaps some crushed chili pistou (see recipe p. 48), if the occasion calls for it.

BROCCOLI, FETA AND ONION FLAN

We tend to make our flans, or quiches, without butter or milk. Olive oil is used for the pastry and soya milk (or a combination of soya and oat milk) is used to make the filling. Adding a little crumbled feta (or basil tofu) makes for a tasty highlight.

Can be DF

For the pastry:

300g / 11 oz plain flour *(or white spelt flour)*
75g / 3 oz olive oil
100ml / 3 ½ fl oz cold water

For the filling:

1-2 onions
1 head of broccoli
1 x 150g packet of feta *(or one packet of basil tofu)*
300ml / 11 fl oz milk *(or a dairy-free alternative)*
3 medium eggs
A small bunch of parsley *(optional)*
25cm / 10" flan tin

Serves 4-6

To MAKE THE PASTRY, put the flour into a bowl with a pinch of salt. Make a dip in the centre and pour in the oil and water. Blend the liquid evenly with the flour, adding some more water if needed, to get a smooth, soft dough. Grease a large, round flan tin and roll the dough out thinly. Press the pastry into the flan tin and trim the edges. Bake the pastry for 10-15 minutes, at 180°C (Fan 160°C) / Gas mark 6, so that it is lightly baked, but not yet coloured.

Cut the onion into thin slices and finely chop the parsley. Cut the broccoli into small florets. Cook the florets in a pan of boiling, salted water. When they are tender, but still bright green, lift them out with a slotted spoon and spread them over a plate, to cool. Warm some oil in a pan and add the onions, plus a pinch of salt. Cook them slowly over a low heat, till soft.

In a bowl, whisk the egg and milk (or soya milk) together, adding the chopped parsley and a good pinch of salt. Spoon the cooked onions into the flan base and layer the broccoli and crumbled feta over the top. Pour in the egg mixture and put the flan in the oven. Bake it at 150°C (Fan 130°C) / Gas mark 5 for 20-30 minutes, till softly set. Leave it to settle for 5-10 minutes before cutting it into wedges, or leave it to cool, if it is intended for later. Serve the flan with a couple of different salads – a simple leafy green salad and a more substantial grain or vegetable salad.

Variations: Swap the broccoli for other vegetables, like strips of grilled or wokked pepper, courgette, or chestnut mushrooms. Roasted squash and cooked spinach or asparagus (if available), also work well.

Tip: For a richer colour and flavour, add a tablespoon of basil pesto or sun-dried tomato paste to the egg and milk mixture for the filling, especially when using non-dairy milk.

VEGETABLE AND SMOKED TOFU STRUDEL

You could use the same pastry and filling to make small individual pastries, or make one large strudel and cut it into thick slices. Serve it with some chunky, braised or roasted vegetables and a rich, dark mushroom gravy (see recipe p. 106).

Can be V, DF

For the pastry:

350g / 12 oz plain flour *(or white spelt flour)*

75g / 3 oz olive oil

125ml / 4 fl oz cold water

For the filling:

1 onion

1 leek *(white part only)*

1-2 stems of celery

1-2 carrots

Half a medium-sized squash *(butternut, hokkaido)*

1 tbsp arrowroot *(or cornflour)*

1 packet of smoked tofu

Serves 4-6

START BY MAKING the filling. Cut the onion, leeks, carrots, celery and squash into small, 'pea-sized' pieces. Warm some oil in a pan and add the onions and leeks, plus a pinch of salt. Cook them over a low heat, till soft. Layer the carrot, celery and squash over the onions. Place a small lid (or a piece of baking parchment) inside the saucepan, directly on top of the vegetables. Cook the vegetables over a very low heat for 10-15 minutes, till tender. Remove the lid (or baking parchment) and add the smoked tofu, cut into small dice. Dissolve the arrowroot in a tablespoon of cold water and stir it into the vegetables and tofu, so that the juices thicken slightly. Leave the filling to cool.

To MAKE THE PASTRY, put the flour into a bowl with a good pinch of salt. Make a dip in the centre and pour in the oil and water. Blend the liquid evenly with the flour, adding some more water if needed, to get a smooth, soft dough. Roll it out thinly, into a large rectangle. Lay it over a greased baking tray and spoon some (or all) of the filling into the centre, leaving enough pastry spare for folding over the top. Wet the edges of the pastry and seal them closed, around the filling. Brush the strudel with a little olive oil. Bake it at 180°C (Fan 160°C) / Gas mark 6, for 35-40 minutes, or till lightly browned.

Tamari and mushroom gravy

This gravy has a deep, rich colour and sweet-savoury flavour. Serve it with roasted vegetables, mashed potatoes and pastry-crusted bakes.

GF, V, DF

1 onion

A few chestnut mushrooms

A few pieces of dried mushroom
   (shitake, porcini, or mixed wild mushrooms)

¼ litre / ½ pint of vegetable stock *(or water)*

A thumbnail-sized piece of ginger *(optional)*

1 tbsp maple syrup *(or agave syrup)*

2-3 tbsp tamari *(or soy sauce)*

1-2 tbsp arrowroot *(or cornflour)*

Makes about ½ litre / 1 pint

PUT THE DRIED MUSHROOMS into a cup and cover them with boiling water. Leave them to soak for half an hour or so, till soft enough to cut into thin slivers. Finely slice the chestnut mushrooms. Cut the onion into thin, half-moon slices and grate the ginger.

WARM SOME OIL in a pan and add the onion, plus a pinch of salt. Cook it over a low heat, till soft. Add the sliced mushrooms (both kinds) and cook them for some minutes more. Add the stock (or water) and the liquid used for soaking the mushrooms. Bring it back to a gentle simmer. Dissolve the arrowroot (or cornflour) in a few tablespoons of cold water. Stir it in, keeping the sauce moving as it thickens. Add the juice pressed from the grated ginger and season it with the maple syrup and tamari. Leave it to simmer for a little longer, allowing the flavours to deepen and become more concentrated.

Crispy sweetcorn polenta

Polenta isn't everyone's cup of tea, but if you are going to make it, make sure that it is well-grilled and golden brown. We add sweetcorn to give it texture and rosemary for extra flavour.

GF, V, DF

250g / 9 oz polenta

1 litre / 1 ¾ pints of water

1 corn on the cob *(or a small tin of sweetcorn)*

A sprig of rosemary *(or 1 tsp dried herbs)*

Serves 4-6

FINELY CHOP THE ROSEMARY and cut the corn on the cob into 2-3 pieces. Cook the corn on the cob for a few minutes, in a small pan of boiling, salted water. Take it out and when cool enough to handle, strip the corn off, using a sharp knife. To make the polenta, pour the water into a large pan and add a good pinch of salt. Tip the polenta into the water and bring it to the boil, stirring it continuously with a whisk. Turn the heat down and keep whisking, allowing the thickened polenta to cook for a minute or two. Stir in the sweetcorn and the finely chopped rosemary (or dried herbs). Scrape the polenta into a shallow, oiled baking dish, spread it out into an even layer and leave it to set.

CUT THE POLENTA INTO LARGE, chunky pieces and place them on a grill tray. Brush them all over with olive oil and turn the grill onto a high setting. Grill the polenta for about 10 minutes, till crispy and well coloured. Turn the pieces over and grill them on the other side. Serve the polenta with a simple tomato sauce, a red kidney bean casserole, or black bean chili and plenty of leafy green salad.

107

108

GREENS

GREENS

AT THE HEART OF GOOD VEGETARIAN COOKING is an understanding that vegetables are an important, even focal, part of a meal. The quality of the vegetables and the way that they are prepared, matters. Beautiful shards of yellow courgette, fine shavings of red cabbage or radish and chunky, oversized pieces of squash, perfectly cooked, can enrich the experience of a dish, without the need for lots of animal protein. Well-prepared vegetables – especially slightly quirky, unusual sorts of vegetable – can take a dish to a whole other level, in quite a simple and inexpensive way.

Novelty isn't the only reason for cooking with a wider variety of vegetables. If the idea is to conserve the goodness and flavour of the vegetables in cooking, then it helps to seek out varieties which are more dense and flavoursome and avoid those which are watery and anemic. At the café, we work a lot with the cooking juices released by vegetables. Rather than adding lots of spices, flavoured sauces and seasonings, we try and dress vegetables as simply as possible – just enough to bring out their best qualities, but not so much that they become overwhelmed by other, stronger flavours.

Relying on vegetables in this way ideally means choosing produce that is grown using organic or biodynamic farming methods, preferably locally. These support the soil fertility of crops and tend to yield produce that is more dense and full of flavour. It is not always possible to buy organic, but anything grown locally, or within a reasonable distance is always preferable to produce that has been air-freighted in from far-flung parts of the world.

Greens

Supermarkets don't make it easy for us to cook with a wide variety of vegetables. Anything green is either tightly cling-filmed, swathed in cellophane, or chopped up and put in plastic trays. Quantities are prescribed by the packaging, not by how much we actually need. Variety is sacrificed in favour of consistency: appearance and shelf-life are the main concern, if fresh fruit and vegetables are to be sold profitably. It's an expensive way of buying vegetables, limited in choice. No wonder that most people, despite the best of intentions, end up with only a handful of usual suspects in their shopping trolley: onions, carrots, potatoes, lettuce and maybe broccoli or spinach.

They may be less convenient, but smaller green-grocers and corner shops, farm shops and market stalls are generally better than supermarkets for buying vegetables. There is usually more variety, less packaging and most things are sold by weight, so that you can decide how much or little you need.

If you can, try buying a week's worth of vegetables from a market stall or grocer shop. Let the vegetables themselves shape how you cook over the next few days. Greens like spinach and lettuces wilt quickly, so they need to be used first. These can give way to green beans and courgettes (in summer), or broccoli and cabbages (in winter), in the middle of the week. Gourds, sweet potatoes and root vegetables might follow them, towards the end of the week. If you can top up your vegetable store with fresh herbs or salad greens, either bought or grown at home, so much the better.

ROASTED ROOT VEGETABLES

We use a marinade of olive oil and umeboshi seasoning, to give the vegetables a slightly tangy flavour.

GF, V, DF

4-5 carrots

1-2 salsify *(or burdock)* roots *(optional)*

3 parsnips

1 small swede

1 bulb of garlic *(optional)*

4-5 tbsp olive oil

1 tsp umeboshi paste

Serves 4-6

PEEL THE CARROTS, salsify (or burdock), parsnips and swede. Remove the centre of the parsnips, if they seem tough. Cut the vegetables into large, chunky strips. Cook them for a few minutes in a pan of boiling, salted water, to soften them. To make the marinade, loosen the umeboshi paste with a little hot water and mix it with the oil and a good pinch of salt.

PUT THE CARROTS, salsify, parsnips and swede into a roasting tin and spoon over the marinade, working it into the vegetables with your fingers. Add the bulb of garlic (still whole). Roast the vegetables at 180°C (Fan 160°C) / Gas mark 6, for about 30-40 minutes, till well-coloured and crispy around the edges. Take out the bulb of garlic and break it into individual cloves. Cut the bases off the cloves and slip them out of their skins. Scatter the roasted garlic cloves among the vegetables and return them to the oven, to warm through.

BRAISED BEETROOT, CARROT
AND SWEET POTATO

In the autumn, you might come across different varieties of beetroot, such as a golden or a variegated pink beetroot. Failing any of these, use a normal beetroot, but keep mixing to a minimum, so that the other vegetables don't all turn purple.

GF, V, DF

4-5 beetroot	A couple of bay leaves
4-5 carrots	A few sprigs of fresh thyme
1 small celeriac *(optional)*	2-3 tbsp balsamic vinegar
1-2 sweet potatoes	4-5 tbsp olive oil

Serves 4-6

WASH THE BEETROOT and cut away the tops and roots. Put them in a pan with plenty of water and cook them for 15-20 minutes, till tender but still quite firm to the touch. Drain the beetroot and when cool enough to handle, slip them out of their skins and cut them into halves or quarters (depending on size).

PEEL THE CARROTS, celeriac and sweet potato. Cut the carrots on the diagonal into 3-4 pieces. Cut the sweet potato and celeriac into large, chunky pieces. Cook the carrot and celeriac in a pan of boiling water for 5 minutes or so, to soften them. Put all the vegetables into a roasting tin and spoon over the vinegar and oil. Add the thyme and bay leaves and a good sprinkling of salt. Cover the vegetables with a sheet of baking parchment and put them in the oven. Cook them at 180°C (Fan 160°C) / Gas mark 6, for about 20-30 minutes, till soft, glossy and sticky-sweet.

BRAISED RED CABBAGE

Pair red cabbage with a warming, wintry dish, like puy lentil and vegetable shepherd's pie, or baked potatoes and red kidney bean casserole.

GF, V, DF

1 small red cabbage

1 red onion

1 apple

2-3 tbsp red wine vinegar

2-3 tbsp apple juice concentrate

A few dried juniper berries *(optional)*

Serves 4-6

CUT THE ONION into thin slices. Wash and finely slice the red cabbage. Peel and core the apple and cut it into slices. Warm some oil in a pan and add the onion, plus a pinch of salt. Cook it over a low heat, till soft. Add the vinegar, apple juice concentrate and the juniper berries. Layer the red cabbage and apple slices over the onions. Add a ladleful of water and a pinch or two of salt. Place a small lid (or a piece of baking parchment) inside the saucepan and directly on top of the red cabbage. Cook it over a low heat for about 40 minutes, till tender.

GRILLED MARINATED MUSHROOMS

Add these succulent mushrooms to salads or sandwiches, or serve them alongside a main dish.

GF, V, DF

150g / 5 oz chestnut mushrooms
2-3 tbsp tamari *(or soy sauce)*
2-3 tbsp olive oil
Half a lemon, juice

CUT THE MUSHROOMS into halves, or leave them whole, depending on size. Put them into a bowl with the tamari, olive oil and lemon juice. Toss them in the marinade, so that they are evenly coated. Leave them to stand for 15 minutes (or longer).

HEAT THE GRILL and spread the mushrooms over a baking tray. Grill the mushrooms for about 10-15 minutes, till well-coloured and juicy.

SAUTÉED GREENS

Cone-shaped spring cabbage is mild in flavour and full of crunch. It is more accessible than some of its more robust cabbage relatives. Adding umiboshi seasoning gives it a slightly tangy flavour, but you could swap it for a little lemon juice and a pinch of salt, to get a similar effect.

GF, V, DF

1-2 heads of spring cabbage
1 tsp umiboshi paste
Sesame oil *(or olive oil)*

Serves 4-6

BREAK OFF THE LEAVES of the spring cabbage and give them a rinse. Remove the spines of the leaves, if they seem tough. Cut the leaves into broad, ribbon-like strips. Cook the cabbage in a pan of boiling, salted water. When it is tender, but still bright green, drain it and spread it over a plate to cool. Dissolve the umiboshi paste in a couple of tablespoons of boiling water.

JUST BEFORE SERVING, heat some sesame oil (or olive oil) in a pan and add the cooked, drained spring cabbage. Stir in the umiboshi seasoning and sauté the greens for a couple of minutes, till they are hot and have taken on a glossy sheen.

VARIATIONS: Swap the spring cabbage for savoy cabbage, sprout tops, or curly kale and prepare them in the same way.

CAVALO NERO SEASONED WITH OLIVE TAPENADE

Cavalo nero has long, pointy, dark green leaves and can be found over the winter months, sold loose at market stalls or small green-grocers. Seasoning it with a small amount of olive tapenade adds a shot of salty, savouriness – a glimpse of summer in the middle of the cold season.

GF, V, DF

300g / 11 oz cavalo nero *(or curly kale)*
2-3 tbsp olive tapenade
Extra virgin olive oil

Serves 4-6

BREAK UP THE CAVALO NERO into individual leaves and give them a rinse. Remove the spines of the leaves, if they seem tough. Cut the leaves into ribbon-like strips. Cook the cavalo nero in a pan of boiling, salted water. When it has lost any toughness and is easy to bite, drain it and spread it over a plate to cool.

LOOSEN THE TAPENADE with a couple of tablespoons of hot water. Just before serving, heat some olive oil in a pan and add the cooked, drained cavalo nero. Stir in the tapenade and sauté the greens for a couple of minutes, till evenly coated and hot.

VARIATIONS: Instead of olive tapenade, add some roasted segments of tomato, or thinly sliced sun-dried tomatoes.

BROCCOLI WITH GINGER
AND SESAME SEEDS

If it is available, use purple sprouting broccoli, otherwise normal broccoli is fine. Leave out the ginger if you prefer to keep it mild.

GF, V, DF

1 head of broccoli
   (or a large bunch of purple sprouting broccoli)
A thumbnail-sized piece of ginger
50g / half a small packet of sesame seeds
Tamari *(or soy sauce)*
Sesame oil *(or sunflower oil)*

Serves 4-6

CUT THE BROCCOLI into small florets. Cook them in a pan of boiling, salted water, for about 1-2 minutes. When they are tender, but still slightly crunchy, lift them out with a slotted spoon and spread them over a plate, to cool.

IN ANOTHER PAN, heat the sesame (or sunflower) oil and add the sesame seeds. As soon as they start to colour, add the drained, cooked broccoli and the ginger. Stir-fry the broccoli for a minute or so, till hot and then season it with tamari (or soy sauce).

CARROTS, BROAD BEANS AND PEPPERS

Take three different vegetables that you like, give them a simple seasoning and you can't go wrong. These three make a pretty combination, with colours of red, orange and muted green.

GF, V, DF

2-3 red peppers

A handful of shelled broad beans

4-5 carrots

Half a lemon, juice

Extra virgin olive oil

Serves 4-6

CUT THE CARROTS IN HALF lengthways and slice them on the diagonal, into large, chunky pieces. Cut the peppers into broad strips and lay them on a baking tray. Add some oil and a pinch of salt and toss them, so that they are evenly coated. Roast them in the oven, for about 15-20 minutes, at 180°C / Gas mark 6.

COOK THE CARROTS and broad beans in a pan of boiling, salted water, for about 5-10 minutes, till tender. Drain them and set them aside. Just before serving, heat some olive oil in a pan and add the cooked carrots and broad beans and the roasted peppers. Heat them through and season them with the lemon juice and a pinch of salt.

CROWD PLEASERS

CROWD PLEASERS

WHETHER IT BE A MILESTONE BIRTHDAY celebration, or just a meal with friends, nothing adds to a sense of occasion more than the food. At such times we tend to opt for rich, meaty foods, like smoked fish, or strong cheeses. But there is no reason why we can't also create delicate morsels and tasty treats, full of vivid colour and flavour, without resorting to meat, fish and dairy products. Keep the selection of snacks simple but full of integrity – we like to include toasted sourdough brochettes, different home-made pates or dips, herby rissoles and spicy caramelised nuts.

CROWD PLEASERS

TOASTED BROCHETTES

Simple, un-fussy and quick to throw together at the last minute, these make ideal food for those occasions that involve milling around with drinks and finger food.

V, DF, can be WF

1 round loaf of bread
  (such as light rye sourdough, or campagne-style bread)
Extra virgin olive oil
2-3 different pates *(see following recipes)*, for toppings

Makes about 20 pieces

CUT THE LOAF of bread into thin slices. Leave the smaller, end pieces whole, but cut the longer ones diagonally, into 2-3 pieces. Lay these on a baking tray and brush them lightly with olive oil. Toast them in the oven, for about 15 minutes, at 150°C (Fan 130°C) / Gas Mark 5. Leave them to cool down and then store them in an airtight container, till needed (they keep well for a day or two).

JUST BEFORE SERVING, spread the toasts with a choice of different pates and arrange them on large plates or trays.

Tip: If you want to go the extra mile, add a piece of garnish to each toast, such as some chopped fresh herbs, slivers of sun-dried tomato or pimento pepper, crumbled feta, or whatever you like, as long as it is in keeping with the base.

HOUMOUS

This is our ever-popular chickpea pate, which we turn out in large quantities at the café.

GF, V, DF

100g / 3 ½ oz dried chickpeas *(or one tin of cooked chickpeas)*

1-2 cloves of garlic

2-3 tbsp tahini

100g / 3 ½ oz extra virgin olive oil

1-2 lemons, juice *(and a little zest – optional)*

1 tsp ground cumin

Makes about 350g / 12 oz

IF YOU ARE USING dried chickpeas, soak them overnight in cold water. Drain them and put them into a pan with plenty of fresh water. Bring them to the boil and cook them for about 45 minutes, till tender. Leave them to cool.

HEAT SOME OIL in a small pan and add the ground cumin. Let it froth for a few seconds and then take it off the heat. Crush the garlic with a pinch of salt. Put the cooked, drained chickpeas into a blender and add the lemon juice, toasted cumin, tahini, crushed garlic and olive oil. Blend it smooth, adding more salt or oil, if needed. Spoon it into a serving dish, add a pinch of cayenne pepper or paprika and trickle some olive oil over the top.

TIP: If you find the raw garlic too strong, try cooking the crushed garlic for a minute or so, in the same pan as the cumin, before adding it to the chickpeas.

125

RED PEPPER, SQUASH

AND CHICKPEA DIP

A version of houmous that we make in the autumn, this is sweeter and a bright orange-red colour.

GF, V, DF

1 red pepper
Half a medium-sized squash *(butternut, hokkaido)*
1 quantity of houmous *(see recipe)*

Makes about 500g / 1 lb

CUT THE SQUASH INTO LARGE, chunky pieces and slice the pepper into broad strips. Lay the pieces of squash and pepper on a baking tray. Add some oil and a pinch of salt and toss them so that they are evenly coated. Put them in the oven and roast them at 150°C (Fan 130°C) / Gas mark 5, for about 20-30 minutes. Make up the houmous as before, but add some (or all) of the roasted squash and red pepper, before blending it smooth.

CARROT AND
THYME PATE

Simple to make, this pate has a sweet, almost smoky flavour, which comes from slow-cooking the onions and carrots, till they almost 'melt'.

GF, V, DF

150g / 5 oz onion *(1-2 onions)*
175g / 6 oz carrots *(about 2-3 carrots)*
A few sprigs of fresh thyme
Extra virgin olive oil

Makes about 300g / 11 oz

PEEL AND SLICE THE ONIONS and carrots. Warm some oil in a pan and add the onion, plus a pinch of salt. Cook it over a low heat, for 5-10 minutes and then add the carrot. Place a small lid (or a piece of baking parchment) inside the saucepan and directly on top of the carrots. Cook the vegetables, in their own juices, over a very low heat, for about half an hour (if not longer). Add a little water if there is a danger of scorching. Finely chop the thyme, removing any woody stems. Put the carrot and onion into a blender, along with 2-3 tbsp of olive oil and blend it smooth. Stir in the chopped thyme and spoon it into a serving dish.

TIP: If you prefer a firmer pate, add some toasted almonds or cashew nuts, when blending the pate.

OLIVE TAPENADE

Spread it onto bread or toast, use it to season sautéed greens, or add it to pasta sauces. Sun-dried tomato paste (also sold as sun-dried tomato 'intense paste') helps to give this olive pate a warmer colour and a sweeter, more rounded flavour.

GF, V, DF

150g / 5 oz black olives
2-3 tbsp sun-dried tomato paste *(optional)*
1-2 cloves of garlic
Half a lemon, juice
2-3 tbsp balsamic vinegar *(optional)*

Makes about 200g / 7 oz

CRUSH THE GARLIC with a pinch of salt and remove the stones from the olives (if they have them). Put the olives into a blender and add the garlic, lemon juice, vinegar and sun-dried tomato paste. Blend it coarsely, adding some olive oil or more lemon juice, if it needs loosening up.

BUTTERBEAN PATE

This is a silky, light pate. The wholegrain mustard gives it sharpness and the white miso adds sweetness and depth of flavour. If miso isn't available, try adding a teaspoon of agave syrup or honey instead.

GF, V, DF

100g / 3 ½ oz dried butterbeans *(or one tin of beans)*

1-2 tsp wholegrain mustard

1 clove of garlic

Half a small red chili *(optional)*

1 tsp white miso *(or agave syrup, or honey)*

1 lemon, juice

75g / 3 oz extra virgin olive oil

Makes about 300g / 11 oz

IF YOU ARE USING dried butterbeans, soak them overnight in cold water. Drain them and put them into a pan with plenty of fresh water. Bring them to the boil and cook them for about 45 minutes, till tender. Leave them to cool.

FINELY CHOP THE GARLIC and the chili. Heat some oil in a small pan and add the garlic and chili, plus a pinch of salt. Cook them for a minute or so. Put the cooked, drained butterbeans into a blender. Add the garlic and chili, along with the mustard, lemon juice, olive oil and white miso (or syrup, or honey). Blend it smooth, adding more salt or oil, if needed. Spoon it into a serving dish, add a pinch of cayenne pepper or paprika, and trickle some olive oil over the top.

SUNFLOWER AND HERB MINI RISSOLES

Serve these gluten-free savoury rice balls with a spicy relish, or alongside a couple of salads, for a light meal. Make sure that you taste the mixture before forming it into rissoles, so that you are happy with the seasoning.

GF, V, DF

150g / 11 oz short-grain brown rice
  (or about 400g / 14 oz cooked rice)
1 onion
1 medium-sized carrot
50g / 2 oz sunflower seeds
1-2 tbsp of sprouting alfalfa seeds *(optional)*
A small bunch of parsley
1 tbsp maple syrup *(or honey)*
1 tbsp tamari
Gram flour *(or rice flour)*, for coating

Makes 20 small rissoles

PUT THE RICE in a pan with twice the amount of water as grain. Cook it over a medium heat, for about 35 minutes, till all the water has been absorbed. Toast the sunflower seeds, by 'dry-roasting' them in a pan over a low heat. When they are evenly coloured, let them cool and then blend them coarsely in a blender (or crush them in a bowl, using the end of a rolling pin).

CHOP THE ONION into very small pieces and finely grate the carrot. Finely chop the parsley. Warm some oil in a small pan and add the onion, plus a pinch of salt. Cook it over a very low heat, till it caramelises. Add the maple syrup and tamari and set it aside.

PUT THE COOKED RICE INTO A BOWL and add the cooked onion, grated carrot, alfalfa, toasted ground sunflower seeds and chopped parsley. Form the mixture into walnut-sized balls. Roll them in a bowl of gram flour (or rice flour), so that they are coated all over.

TAKE A LARGE frying pan and pour in about 1 cm / ½" oil. When the oil is hot, fry the rissoles in batches of 6-7, rolling them once in a while, so that they colour all over. Lift them out with a spatula and set them on some kitchen paper. Serve them straight away, or keep them for later, when they may be warmed through in the oven.

VARIATION: Swap half of the rice for millet or quinoa, or another grain.

SPICY CARAMELISED NUTS

Vary the nuts according to what you like. Use just one kind, or a mixture of different ones. Sprinkle the nuts over salads or main dishes, or just snack on them, as they are.

GF, V, DF

A handful each of brazil nuts, hazelnuts, almonds
    and cashew nuts
4 tbsp tamari *(or soy sauce)*
2-3 tbsp rice syrup *(or honey)*
A pinch of cayenne pepper

RINSE THE NUTS, by putting them into a sieve and running them under cold water. Spread them over a baking tray and toast them in the oven for 30-35 minutes, at 150°C (Fan 130°C) / Gas mark 5, taking them out and turning them with a spatula once or twice, so that they colour evenly.

MIX THE TAMARI, SYRUP AND CAYENNE pepper together and spoon it over the nuts. Stir them, so as to coat them evenly. Return the tray to the oven for another five minutes, to dry them out a little. Once cool, fork through the nuts, to break up any clusters.

SUNDAY BRUNCH

SUNDAY BRUNCH

WHEN WE STARTED OPENING for brunch on a Sunday, it wasn't immediately clear what we would serve. The macrobiotic approach would have been to serve miso soup, but somehow, we felt, many of us were not quite ready for this. Continental breakfast seemed like a good idea, until we discovered how impractical it was to prepare all the brioches, pastries and so on in advance, given how busy weekends can be. So we finally settled on our own version of a few cooked breakfast classics, like mushrooms on toast and poached or scrambled egg, as well as some basics, like porridge and granola. Most of these can be rustled up in minutes, just as breakfast ought to be.

CREAMY PORRIDGE

We make our dairy-free porridge with a combination of rice milk and oat milk. The rice milk brings sweetness and the oat milk brings creaminess.

WF, V, DF

One handful of porridge oats per person
Oat milk *(optional)*
Rice milk *(optional)*
Maple syrup, to serve

PUT THE OATS INTO A PAN with a pinch of salt and just enough water to cover. Leave them to soak for 15 minutes (or longer). To make the porridge, add enough oat milk and/or rice milk, so that the oats move freely when stirred. Slowly bring it to the boil and let it simmer on a low heat for 10-15 minutes. Add more oat or rice milk, if the porridge needs loosening. Spoon it into bowls and serve it with maple syrup and some more oat or rice milk.

Granola

This tastes good with milk (or a dairy-free alternative), or as a crunchy topping for yoghurt and fruit compote. We also use granola for making our ever-popular monster cookies (see recipe, p. 164).

WF, V, DF

450g / 14 oz porridge oats

¼ tsp salt

½ tsp cinnamon

125g / 4 oz nuts

(a mixture of cashew nuts, almonds and hazelnuts)

75g / 3 oz sunflower seeds

75g / 3 oz barley malt syrup

100g / 3 ½ oz rice syrup *(or agave syrup)*

100g / 3 ½ oz sunflower oil

Makes about 900g / 2 lb

PUT THE OATS into a large bowl. Stir in the salt, cinnamon, nuts and seeds. In a separate bowl, mix the barley malt syrup, rice syrup and oil and pour it onto the oats, nuts and seeds. Work it evenly into the oat mixture, using your hands. Scrape it into a deep roasting tin and place it in the oven. Toast the granola at 150°C (Fan 130°C) / Gas mark 5, for about 45 minutes, taking it out occasionally and stirring it with a spatula, to break up any lumps. When ready, it will have coloured slightly, but still be a little moist – it will harden and dry out further as it cools down.

Spiced fruit compote

Serve this warm or cold, with yoghurt or cream (or a dairy-free alternative).

GF, V, DF

100g / 3 ½ oz dried apricots
  (un-sulphured, if available)
100g / 3 ½ oz dried figs
50g / 2 oz sultanas
50g / 2 oz dried cranberries or blueberries
1 cinnamon stick *(or ¼ tsp cinnamon)*
½ tsp mixed spice
300ml / 11 fl oz water
1 orange *(or lemon)*

Wash the orange (or lemon) and use a peeler to pare away 2-3 long strips of peel. Cut the figs in half, removing the stalks. Cut the apricots in half and put them in a pan with the figs, sultanas and cranberries. Add the water, cinnamon stick, orange citrus peel and mixed spice and bring it to the boil.

Turn down the heat and let it simmer for 10-15 minutes, till the fruit becomes tender. Let it cool and allow the fruit to steep in its cooking liquid, so that the flavours of the spices and citrus peel are passed on to the fruit.

Mushrooms on toast

We use our home-made sourdough bread for this breakfast classic. It adds a strong tangy flavour of its own and turns very crunchy when toasted. Failing sourdough, or a campagne-style bread, any kind of bread would be fine.

Can be WF, V, DF

200g / 7 oz chestnut mushrooms
1-2 tbsp soy sauce *(shoyu)*
1-2 slices of bread per person
A small bunch of parsley *(optional)*
A few sprigs of fresh thyme
    (optional – but it makes for a Rolls Royce version)

Serves 2-4

FINELY SLICE THE MUSHROOMS, cutting them in half first if they are very large. Finely chop the parsley and thyme. Heat some oil in a large frying pan and add the mushrooms. Keep the heat up and stir the mushrooms often, to stop them from catching.

WHEN THEY are tender, stir in the soy sauce and the chopped thyme. Turn the heat up to drive off any juices and as soon as the mushrooms start to fry rather than simmer, they are done. Pile the mushrooms onto the slices of toasted bread and scatter the chopped parsley over the top.

Poached egg on toast

People prefer their eggs done in different ways; we cook them so that they are firm to the touch, but still have a soft, liquid yolk.

Can be WF, DF

1-2 eggs per person
1-2 slices of bread per person
Salt and vinegar
  (cider or white wine vinegar), for poaching
Coarse salt and ground black pepper, to serve

Fill a large saucepan with about 2 litres / 4 pints of water. Bring it to the boil and stir in 1-2 tbsp vinegar and about half a teaspoon of salt. Turn the heat down, so that it stays at a steady simmer and give the water a swirl with a whisk. Break the eggs as close to the surface of the water as possible, letting them slide in gently. Use a slotted spoon to lift them out after 3-4 minutes. Toast the slices of bread and trickle some olive oil over them. Lay the poached eggs on top and season them with a pinch salt and some freshly ground black pepper.

'EGG IN A NEST'

We make our own bagels for this Star Anise speciality (see recipe, p. 173), but if you prefer, use ready-made bagels.

DF

2 eggs per person
1 bagel per person
Olive oil

SLICE THE BAGELS IN HALF. Heat some oil in a frying pan and lay the bagels, cut side down, in the pan. Break an egg into the middle of each bagel half. Lightly season them with salt and let them cook for a couple of minutes. Carefully flip them over, using a spatula and cook them briefly on the other side. Season them with some freshly ground black pepper.

Dennis eating mushrooms on Sourdough toast—

141

SWEET TREATS

MONSTER COOKIES £1·80
(VEGAN & WHEAT FREE)

CRANBERRY & VANILLA
COOKIES   £1·20
(VEGAN & WHEAT)

ORANGE & CHOCOLATE
SPIRAL COOKIES £1·20
(VEGAN)

CHOCOLATE & HAZELNUT
COOKIES   £1·20
(VEGAN & WHEAT FREE)

SWEET TREATS

ALL THE CAKES AND COOKIES that we serve at the café are baked in-house. Over the years, we have settled on a core of popular recipes, but we also like to surprise people every now and then and try out something different. We prefer to use foods in their most natural form in baking, such as oil instead of margarine and unrefined syrups instead of sugar. Nuts, seeds and fruit are used a lot, as well as oat flakes and different flours, like rye, spelt and rice flour.

Our cakes and cookies are made without refined sugar. We are aware of being surrounded today by snacks and confectionary that contain very high levels of refined sugar. This can create all kinds of problems, both health-related and social, especially among children. The café tries to provide an alternative to these high-sugar snacks. We do this by using unrefined sweeteners, like rice syrup, agave syrup, barley malt syrup, maple syrup and honey. These are more slow-burning than refined sugar and don't cause the same 'sugar rush'.

We are being asked more and more to offer cakes and biscuits which take into account diet restrictions, by people who have an intolerance to dairy, wheat or gluten. Many of our cakes and almost all of our cookies, are made without dairy products or eggs. And as a rule, we try to include cakes and cookies made with oats, spelt flour, or gluten-free flour, alongside those we make with wheat flour.

Cakes and slices

Our cakes are mainly based on one simple 'soda cake' recipe. In essence, it involves flour, syrup, fruit juice, sunflower oil, baking powder and salt. Whatever else is added, the proportions of these basic ingredients stay much the same, whether it be a carrot cake, or a chocolate cake. For the sake of simplicity, the syrup in these recipes is usually given as one single quantity. In practice, we use a blend of two or three syrups, including up to a quarter of barley malt syrup. This gives a malty taste and a darker crumb to our cakes and biscuits. But syrup is syrup and one kind can be fairly easily swapped for another.

Apart from being free of dairy products and refined sugar, the good thing about these cakes is that they are straightforward and quick to make. Dry ingredients are measured into one bowl and liquid ingredients into another. The two are then mixed together and poured into a baking tin and baked until firm to the touch. It is important with soda cakes not to over-cook them, or they can become dry and crumbly. When baked just right, they have moist and slightly chewy texture.

In the absence of icing sugar or cream, we try to find other ways of decorating a cake. Sometimes, all that is needed is a light glaze, like some apricot conserve (100% fruit) brushed over the top. For a richer cake, we might make a cashew or almond cream, or a dairy and sugar-free chocolate icing. Our one guilty pleasure is a coffee buttercream, that we make with maple syrup and good organic butter, which we use for covering our coffee walnut cake.

146

CARROT AND SULTANA CAKE

Cover this cake with a simple apricot glaze, or split it in half and fill it with a rich cashew cream (see recipe, p. 151) as well.

V, DF

75g / 3 oz carrot, finely grated
50g / 2 oz sultanas
200g / 7 oz plain white flour
1½ level tsp baking powder
½ level tsp cinnamon
200g / 7 oz rice syrup *(or agave syrup)*
60ml / 2 ½ fl oz orange juice
60g / 2 ½ oz sunflower oil
Apricot conserve *(such as Meridian, 100% fruit),* to glaze
20cm / 8" round cake tin, greased and lined

Serves 6-8

PEEL AND FINELY GRATE the carrots. Put the flour, baking powder, cinnamon and a pinch of salt into a bowl. In a separate bowl, mix the syrup with the orange juice and oil. Pour it onto the flour, along with the grated carrot and sultanas. Lightly stir it together and scrape the mixture into the cake tin. Bake it at 180°C (Fan 160°C) / Gas mark 6, for 30-40 minutes, till firm to the touch. Brush the top with some apricot conserve, to give it a sticky glaze.

TIP: For a cake with a deeper colour and a slightly malty taste, swap a quarter of the rice syrup (or agave syrup) for barley malt syrup.

CHOCOLATE CAKE

A dark and moist chocolate cake, but without the usual dairy, eggs and refined sugar.

V, DF

180g / 6 oz plain flour
30g / 1 oz cocoa powder
1½ tsp baking powder
200g / 7 oz rice syrup *(or agave syrup)*
100ml / 3 ½ fl oz orange juice
60g / 2 oz sunflower oil
20cm / 8" round cake tin, greased and lined

For the chocolate icing:

4 tbsp cocoa powder
4-5 tbsp rice syrup *(or agave syrup)*
A few squares of dark chocolate *(dairy-free)*, to decorate

Serves 6-8

SIFT THE FLOUR AND COCOA powder into a bowl. Add the baking powder and a pinch of salt. In a separate bowl, mix the syrup with the orange juice and oil. Pour it onto the flour and cocoa powder and lightly whisk it together. Scrape the mixture into the cake tin. Bake it at 180°C (Fan 160°C) / Gas mark 6, for 30-35 minutes, till firm to the touch.

To make the chocolate icing, put the cocoa powder and syrup into a bowl. Work the syrup into the cocoa powder with the back of a spoon, adding a teaspoon or two of hot water if needed, to make a thick, creamy icing. Spread the icing over the cake and cover the top with grated, dark chocolate.

Variations: For a richer, more fudge-like chocolate cake, melt a quarter of a 100g bar of dark chocolate and stir it into the cake mixture. Add the grated zest of an orange to the cake mixture, for a chocolate and orange version.

GLUTEN-FREE APPLE AND ALMOND CAKE

Fresh fruit and ground almonds help to soften the edges of the gluten-free flour. Fill the cake with almond cream (see recipe, p. 151), or fruit conserve, or just serve it as it is.

GF, DF

2 medium-sized apples

200g / 7 oz rice syrup *(or agave syrup)*

125g / 4 oz dairy-free margarine

2 medium eggs

150g / 5 oz gluten-free plain flour *(such as Dove's Farm)*

75g / 3 oz ground almonds

1 ½ level tsp baking powder

½ tsp mixed spice

Maple syrup *(or honey)*, to glaze

20cm / 8" round cake tin, greased and lined

Serves 6–8

PEEL THE APPLES and cut them into quarters, taking out the cores. Finely grate two apple quarters and cut the rest into thin slices. Put the syrup and margarine into a bowl and beat them together, till creamy. Add the eggs and whisk them in. Stir in the gluten-free flour, grated apple and ground almonds, baking powder, mixed spice and a pinch of salt. Gently fold in the apple slices. Scrape the mixture into a cake tin. Bake it at 180°C (Fan 160°C) / Gas mark 6, for 30-35 minutes, or till firm to the touch. Brush the cake with maple syrup (or honey), while still warm from the oven.

ALMOND OR CASHEW CREAM

Use this for filling cakes like the gluten-free apple and almond cake, or carrot cake. Toasting the nuts first gives the cream a better colour and flavour.

GF, V, DF

100g / 5 oz blanched almonds *(or cashew nuts)*

2-3 tbsp rice syrup *(or agave syrup)*

250ml / 12 fl oz rice milk *(or soya milk)*

1-2 tbsp sunflower oil

TOAST THE ALMONDS (or cashew nuts), by putting them on a baking tray in the oven, for about 10 minutes, at 150°C (Fan 130°C) / Gas mark 5. Transfer the toasted nuts to a small pan and add the rice milk (or soya milk). Bring it to the boil, cover it with a lid and let it simmer gently for 10-15 minutes, till the nuts are tender. Leave them to cool.

TIP THE almonds (or cashew nuts) into a blender, adding a little of the cooking liquid. Spoon in the syrup and the oil. Blend it smooth, adding extra liquid if needed, to get a thick, spreadable consistency. Store the cream in the fridge, if you are not using it straightaway. It will stay fresh for several days, if kept chilled.

Coffee and walnut cake

This is the exception that proves the rule – far from dairy-free, we serve this cake covered in a layer of rich coffee buttercream.

100g / 3 ½ oz walnut halves or pieces

200g / 7 oz plain flour

1½ tsp baking powder

200g / 5 oz rice syrup *(or agave syrup)*

1 medium egg

75ml / 3 fl oz espresso *(or strong instant coffee)*

60g / 2 oz vegetable oil

20cm / 8" round cake tin, greased and lined

For the coffee buttercream:

100g / 3 ½ oz butter, softened

3-4 tbsp maple syrup *(or other light syrup)*

Espresso *(or strong instant coffee)*

Serves 6–8

Toast the walnuts, by putting them on a tray in the oven, for about 15 minutes, at 180°C (Fan 160°C) / Gas mark 6. When cool, put the walnuts into a bowl and crush them roughly, using the end of a rolling pin. Add the flour, baking powder and a pinch of salt to the crushed walnuts. In a separate bowl, mix the oil, syrup and coffee. Beat in the egg and pour it onto the flour and walnuts. Lightly stir it together and scrape the mixture into the cake tin. Bake it at 180°C (Fan 160°C) / Gas mark 6, for 35-40 minutes, till firm to the touch.

To MAKE THE COFFEE BUTTERCREAM, mix the butter with the syrup. Gradually add the coffee, beating in a spoonful at a time, till you have a silky, spreadable consistency. Cover the top and sides of the cake with the buttercream and decorate it with a few toasted walnut halves.

VARIATION: Swap the walnuts for hazelnuts and replace the coffee in the cake mixture with orange juice. This cake can be made without egg, by increasing the liquid to 100ml / 3 ½ fl oz.

Pear and almond frangipane

Poaching the pears beforehand, means that they are meltingly soft and won't discolour after baking.

V, DF

For the pastry:

  150g / 5 oz plain flour

  ¼ tsp baking powder

  60g / 2 oz rice syrup *(or agave syrup)*

  75g / 3 oz dairy-free margarine

For the frangipane:

  4-5 ripe pears

  75g / 3 ½ oz plain flour

  75g / 3 ½ oz ground almonds

  ¼ tsp baking powder

  75g / 3 oz rice syrup *(or agave syrup)*

  3 tbsp orange juice

  3 tbsp sunflower oil

  1-2 tbsp apricot conserve

    (such as Meridian, 100% fruit), to glaze

  One 23cm/9" round flan tin, greased and lined

Serves 6-8

Peel the pears and put them (whole) into a pan, with enough water to just cover them. Bring it to the boil and let it simmer for 10-15 minutes, till the pears are tender. Drain them and leave them to cool.

To MAKE the pastry, put the flour, baking powder and a pinch of salt into a bowl. Add the margarine and rub it into the flour. Stir in the syrup and work it into a soft, crumbly dough. Roll it out and press it into the flan tin, trimming the edges.

To MAKE THE FRANGIPANE filling, put the flour, ground almonds and baking powder into a bowl. Stir in the syrup, orange juice and oil. Spread the filling over the base of the flan. Cut the pears into quarters (removing the cores) and arrange them over the filling.

PUT THE flan into the oven, on a low shelf (this helps ensure that the base is well cooked). Bake it at 180°C (Fan 160°C) / Gas mark 6, for 35-40 minutes, or till the pastry starts to colour and the frangipane feels firm to the touch. Brush it all over with apricot conserve, to give it a sticky glaze.

DATE AND OAT SLICE

Soft stewed dates, sandwiched between layers of spiced oat crumble.

V, DF, WF

For the date filling:
300g / 11 oz dates
200ml / 7 oz water

For the oat crumble:
360g / 12 ½ oz porridge oats
100g / 3 ½ oz sunflower oil
120g / 4 oz rice syrup *(or agave syrup)*
½ tsp mixed spice
23cm/9" square cake tin, or a small roasting tin, greased and lined

Makes 10-12 pieces

PUT THE DATES INTO A PAN with the water and let them simmer for 5-10 minutes, till soft. Roughly blend the dates (including the cooking liquid), using a blender. To make the oat crumble, mix the porridge oats with the mixed spice and a pinch of salt. Add the syrup and the oil and work the ingredients together into a crumbly, sticky mixture.

TIP HALF THE OAT CRUMBLE into the baking tin and press it into an even, compact layer. Spread the date mixture carefully over the base and scatter the rest of the oat crumble over the top. Bake it at 150°C (Fan 130°C) / Gas mark 5, for 30-40 minutes, till the oat crumble begins to colour slightly, around the edges.

VARIATION: To make an apricot and oat slice, swap the dates for dried apricots and prepare it in the same way.

Honey, fruit and seed flapjack

Using a blend of honey and rice syrup means that you can be more sparing with the honey. It also ensures that the flavour of the honey is not too overbearing.

V, DF, WF

300g / 11 oz porridge oats

100g / 3 ½ oz seeds *(pumpkin, sunflower, sesame)*

1 tbsp golden linseeds *(optional)*

50g / 1 ½ oz sultanas

50g / 1 ½ oz dried cranberries *(optional)*

100g / 3 ½ oz honey

160g / 5 oz rice syrup *(or agave syrup)*

90g / 3 ½ oz sunflower oil

23cm/9" square baking tin, greased and lined

Makes 10-12 pieces

PUT THE OATS INTO a large mixing bowl with the seeds, sultanas, cranberries and a pinch of salt. Add the honey, syrup and oil and work them in evenly, with your fingers. Tip the mixture into the baking tin and press it into a compact layer. Bake it at 150°C / Gas mark 5 for 30-40 minutes, or till it begins to colour slightly, around the edges. Leave it to cool before cutting it into chunky squares.

Sweet treats

We like our cookies crunchy on the outside, but soft and slightly chewy on the inside. Spelt flour is used in many of our cookies and gives them a soft, crumbly texture. The unrefined syrups that we use, mean that the cookies are less sweet than if we were to make them with sugar and this allows other flavours to shine through.

Many of our cookies, like our cakes, are loosely based on one simple idea, which can be varied by adding fruit, nuts, seeds, vanilla, spices and so on. This means a batch of cookies can be made with very little fuss. The dough is quickly made by mixing flour, baking powder, sunflower oil or margarine and a blend of syrups. It is portioned up, shaped by hand and baked there and then. No mixers and hardly any waste or mess (very practical in a small, hectic kitchen).

The cookies in this book have been scaled down in size. We make our cookies palm-sized, but then our baking trays are large and so is our oven. Making them smaller means that they fit more easily onto ordinary baking trays and are quicker to bake. But if you like them as we make them, by all means make them larger and give them a little longer in the oven. Take care not to overbake the cookies: they need to be still soft when they leave the oven, as they will firm up as they cool down.

CRANBERRY AND VANILLA COOKIES

Cranberries and vanilla work well together, but if you prefer, swap the cranberries for sultanas or raisins.

V, DF, WF

300g / 11 oz white spelt flour *(or plain white flour)*
1 tsp baking powder
75g / 3 oz dried cranberries
200g / 5 oz rice syrup *(or agave syrup)*
75g / 3 oz dairy-free margarine
4 tbsp sunflower oil
1 tsp vanilla extract

Makes about 16

PUT THE FLOUR, baking powder and a pinch of salt into a bowl. Add the margarine and rub it into the flour. In a separate bowl, mix the syrup with the oil and vanilla extract. Pour the mixture onto the flour, add the cranberries and work it into a soft dough.

DIVIDE THE dough into walnut-sized pieces. Flatten them into rounds and place them on a lined baking tray, leaving enough space between cookies for them to spread a little. Bake them at 150°C (Fan 130°C) / Gas mark 5, for 15-20 minutes, till lightly coloured.

Chocolate and hazelnut cookies

V, DF, WF

150g / 5 oz white spelt flour *(or plain white flour)*
150g / 5 oz wholemeal spelt flour *(or plain wholemeal flour)*
30g / 1 oz cocoa powder
75g / 3 oz hazelnuts
1 tsp baking powder
250g / 9 oz rice syrup *(or agave syrup)*
100g / 3 ½ oz dairy-free margarine
4 tbsp sunflower oil

Makes about 20

Toast the hazelnuts, by putting them on a baking tray in the oven for about 10 minutes, at 150°C (Fan 130°C) / Gas mark 5. Once they have cooled, grind them coarsely in a blender. Sift the flour and cocoa powder into a bowl. Stir in the ground hazelnuts, baking powder and a pinch of salt. Add the margarine and rub it in. In a separate bowl, mix the syrup and oil. Pour it onto the flour and work it into a soft dough.

Divide the dough into walnut-sized portions. Flatten them into rounds and place them on a baking tray, leaving enough space between cookies for them to spread a little. Bake them at 150°C (Fan 130°C) / Gas mark 5, for 15-20 minutes.

Tip: Roasted, ground hazelnuts is available ready-prepared, in some healthfood shops. Alternatively, you could use ground almonds.

Almond biscotti

Our version of the traditional Italian twice-baked biscuit.

V, DF

300g / 11 oz plain flour

75g / 3 oz blanched, whole almonds

50g / 2 ½ oz sultanas

1 tsp baking powder

150g / 5 oz rice syrup *(or agave syrup)*

50g / 2 ½ oz maple syrup

100g / 3 ½ oz dairy-free margarine

4 tbsp sunflower oil

Makes 12-15 pieces

Toast the almonds, by putting them on a baking tray in the oven for about 10 minutes, at 150°C (Fan 130°C) / Gas mark 5. Put the flour, baking powder and a pinch of salt into a bowl. Add the margarine and rub it in. In a separate bowl, mix the oil and syrups. Pour the mixture onto the flour, adding the toasted almonds and sultanas and work it into a soft dough. Scrape the dough onto a lined baking tray. Shape it into a long, flat loaf-shape, about a hand's width wide and two finger-widths thick. Bake it at 150°C (Fan 130°C) / Gas mark 5, for 20-30 minutes.

When it starts to puff up and feel firm to the touch, take it out and leave it to cool slightly. Using a sharp serrated knife, cut the loaf into generous slices. Lay the slices on a baking tray, cut side down. Return them to the oven and bake them for a further 15 minutes or so, till the cut edges start to turn crisp.

161

Gluten-free brazil nut and chocolate chip cookies

Toasted ground brazil nuts give this gluten-free cookie a rich flavour and crumbly texture. The dough is very sticky, so it can either be spooned onto the baking tray to make free-form cookies, or it can be rolled up in baking parchment, frozen solid and then sliced into rounds.

GF, DF

300g / 11 oz gluten-free plain flour *(Dove's Farm)*
180g / 6 oz brazil nuts
1 tsp baking powder
125g / 4 oz dairy-free margarine
260g / 9 oz rice syrup *(or agave syrup)*
2 medium eggs
50g / 2 oz dark chocolate *(dairy-free)*

Makes about 20

TOAST THE BRAZIL NUTS, by putting them on a baking tray in the oven for about 15 minutes, at 150°C (Fan 130°C) / Gas mark 5. When they have cooled, grind them coarsely, using a blender. Put the gluten-free flour, ground brazil nuts, baking powder and a pinch of salt into a bowl. Add the margarine and rub it in. Stir in the syrup and the eggs, along with the chopped chocolate.

DROP LARGE SPOONFULS of the mixture onto a lined baking tray, leaving some space between the cookies, for them to spread. Flatten them slightly with the back of a spoon (dip it in water to stop the dough sticking to it). Bake them at 150°C (Fan 130°C) / Gas mark 5, for 15-20 minutes, till lightly coloured.

162

GINGERBREAD MEN

A good one for getting children involved in baking.

V, DF

300g / 11 oz plain flour

½ tsp baking powder

1-2 tsp ground ginger

100g / 3 ½ oz dairy-free margarine

200g / 7 oz rice syrup *(or agave syrup)*

Makes about 20

PUT THE FLOUR, baking powder, ginger and a pinch of salt into a bowl. Add the margarine and rub it into the flour. Stir in the syrup and work it into a smooth dough. Put the dough in the fridge for half an hour or so, to firm up.

ROLL OUT THE DOUGH to about ½ cm thickness. Cut out gingerbread men (or other shapes), using a biscuit cutter and lay them onto lined baking trays. Bake them at 150°C (Fan 130°C) / Gas mark 5, for 10-12 minutes, till lightly coloured. Leave them to cool and then decorate them with piped chocolate, if you like.

Monster cookies

With their distinctive aniseed flavour and generous amounts of toasted nuts and seeds, these are a best-seller at the cafe.

V, DF, WF

200g / 7 oz granola*

100g / 3 ½ oz white spelt flour *(or plain white flour)*

100g / 3 ½ oz wholemeal spelt flour *(or plain wholemeal flour)*

1 tsp baking powder

½ tsp cinnamon

¼ tsp ground star anise

100g / 3 ½ oz rice syrup *(or agave syrup)*

50g / 2 oz barley malt syrup

75g / 3 oz sunflower oil

2-3 tbsp orange juice

Makes about 20

Put the flours, baking powder, spices and a pinch of salt into a bowl and stir in the granola. In a separate bowl, mix the syrups with the orange juice and oil. Pour it onto the flour and granola and work it into a soft dough. Divide the dough into walnut-sized portions. Flatten them into rounds and place them onto lined baking trays. Bake them at 150°C (Fan 130°C) / Gas mark 5, for 15-20 minutes, till lightly coloured.

* To make granola, follow our recipe (see recipe, p. 137). Alternatively, use 125g / 4 oz of ready-made, plain oat granola and add a small handful each of whole almonds, hazelnuts and cashew nuts.

Fig and coconut chocolate balls

Half-dipped in dark chocolate and sprinkled with coconut, these make a tasty (but healthy) chocolate treat.

V, DF, WF

125g / 4 oz dried figs

100g / 3 ½ oz desiccated coconut

100g / 3 ½ oz porridge oats

2 tbsp cocoa powder

75g / 3 oz rice syrup *(or agave syrup)*

40g / 1 ½ oz sunflower oil

A few squares of dark chocolate *(dairy-free)*, to decorate

Makes about 15

TOAST THE COCONUT, by spreading it over a tray and putting it in the oven for 10 minutes, at 150°C (Fan 130°C) / Gas mark 5. Put the figs into a pan, removing any tough bits of stalk. Add enough water to just cover them and let them simmer for 10-15 minutes, till tender. Blend the figs coarsely (including the cooking liquid), using a blender. Put the oats, toasted coconut, cocoa powder and a pinch of salt into a bowl. Stir in the fig purée, syrup and oil.

FORM THE MIXTURE into walnut-sized balls and place them on a lined baking tray. Bake them at 150°C (Fan 130°C) / Gas mark 5, for 20-25 minutes. Leave them to cool, before decorating them.

MELT THE CHOCOLATE in a bowl placed over a pan of simmering water. Dip the fig balls in the chocolate, to half-coat them. Sprinkle a little desiccated coconut on the top and put them aside, till the chocolate has set.

165

DAILY BREAD

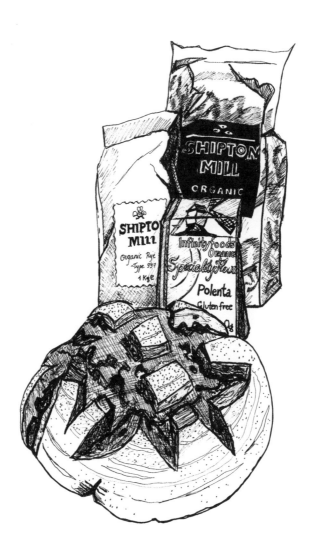

DAILY BREAD

BAKING BREAD AND PASTRIES is one of the first jobs of the day at the café. It is something we do, without fail, everyday. The dough for our bread and croissants is all prepared the day before and left to rise overnight. There is one white yeasted dough for rolls, paninis, focaccia and the like. There is also a sourdough, made sometimes with just rye flour, but often with a mixture of rye and white flour, for our round, crusty sourdough loaves. And finally there is an enriched dough, which is used for all the croissants and pastries.

We favour using fresh yeast over dried, in our yeasted doughs. It is less potent and gives the bread a better flavour. Fresh yeast is available from small bakeries and healthfood shops, although you may need to ask for it over the counter. Make sure it is creamy smooth and pale in colour, as there is nothing quite like tired yeast to ruin a batch of bread dough (this is why people use dried yeast). Try allowing the dough plenty of time to rise the first time round, rather than rushing it into the oven. By giving it time to mature in the traditional way, our bread is more digestible, more moist and gains a better texture.

Sourdough bread is different from yeasted bread because it uses a mixture of fermented flour and water to leaven the bread, instead of fresh or dried yeast. Baking a loaf of sourdough bread is just one part of a cycle, which involves keeping and feeding a sourdough 'starter'. In our kitchen, we have two sourdough starters, or 'mothers' as they are called. One is made with rye flour and the other with wheat flour and they bubble away quietly, in their tubs, in the fridge. Feeding them is fairly empirical. After we have taken out a portion to make the main bread dough, we replenish the starter with more flour and water. We don't measure them exactly: it is enough to go by texture. If it feels thick and porridge-like when stirred, it is about right.

You can make a starter from scratch by mixing flour and water and leaving it for a few days, till it begins to ferment. Be aware that it takes some time for a new starter to become really lively and yield bread that has volume and lightness.

Overnight-leavened bread

This basic white bread dough can be used in so many different ways, for making loaves, bread rolls, pizza, flatbread and the like.

V, DF

600g / 1 lb 6 oz organic strong white bread flour

1½ level tsp salt

A thumbnail-sized piece of fresh yeast

   (or 1 level tsp dried yeast)

400ml / 14 fl oz water

2-3 tbsp olive oil

Makes one large loaf

Put the flour, salt and oil in a large mixing bowl. Dissolve the fresh yeast in a little of the water. Pour the yeast and liquid onto the flour and mix it to a soft dough. Knead the dough for 5-10 minutes, till smooth. Put it back into the mixing bowl, coating it with more olive oil. Cover the bowl with a damp tea towel and leave it to rise at room temperature, for several hours, or overnight.

Turn the dough out of the bowl and shape it into a ball, tucking the dough underneath itself, to create a taught surface. Place it on a greased, floured tray. Cover it with a damp tea-towel again and leave it to rise for an hour or so. Preheat the oven to 220°C (Fan 200°C) / Gas mark 7. Put the bread into the oven and bake it for 35-40 minutes, turning the oven down to 180°C (Fan 160°C) / Gas mark 6, after the first 15 minutes. When fully-baked, the loaf will be evenly coloured and feel hard to the touch.

ROSEMARY FOCACCIA

V, DF

ADD SOME CHOPPED FRESH ROSEMARY to the basic overnight-leavened bread dough mixture. After the dough has risen, turn it out of the bowl and divide it into two pieces. Roll them out into large rectangles, about a finger-width's thickness and place them onto two greased, floured baking trays. Let the dough rest for 15-20 minutes. Using your fingertips, prod the dough, so as to make lots of little holes all over the surface. Trickle some olive oil over the dough and sprinkle it with more chopped rosemary and some coarsely-ground salt (if you like). Bake the focaccia in a pre-heated oven at 220°C (Fan 200°C) / Gas mark 7 for 20-25 minutes, till it starts to colour.

ROSEMARY

PITTA BREAD

V, DF

MAKE ONE QUANTITY of the basic overnight-leavened bread dough. After the dough has risen, turn it out of the bowl and divide it into egg-sized pieces. Roll each piece into a long, oval shape, about a half a finger-width's thickness. Place these onto greased, floured baking trays and let them rest for 15-20 minutes. Bake the pitta bread in a pre-heated oven at 220°C (Fan 200°C) / Gas mark 7 for 15-20 minutes, or till they have ballooned in size.

172

BAGELS

Bagels get their shiny crust and chewy texture from being plunged into a pan of simmering, salted water for a few seconds, just before they go into the oven.

V, DF

600g / 1 lb 6 oz organic strong white bread flour
1½ level tsp salt
A thumbnail-sized piece of fresh yeast *(or 1 level tsp dried yeast)*
400ml / 14 fl oz water

Makes 8-10 bagels

PUT THE FLOUR AND SALT in a large mixing bowl. Dissolve the fresh yeast in a little of the water. Pour the yeast and liquid onto the flour and mix it to a soft dough. Knead the dough for 5-10 minutes, till smooth. Put the dough back into the mixing bowl. Coat it with a little olive oil and cover it with a damp cloth. Leave it to rise for 2-3 hours at room temperature.

TO MAKE THE BAGELS, spread a tea towel out on a work surface and dust it generously with flour. Divide the dough into 8-10 pieces and shape them into balls. Poke a hole through each one using a finger and stretch it evenly to make a ring shape. Lay the rings on the floured tea towel and leave them to rise for about 30 minutes. Meanwhile, fill a large saucepan with about 2 litres / 4 pints of water. Add 1 tbsp of salt and bring it to the boil. Use a large slotted spoon to lower each bagel into the water (which should be kept at a steady simmer). Count to five and then lift the bagel out and place it on a greased baking tray. Bake the bagels in a pre-heated oven at 200°C (Fan 180°C) / Gas mark 7, for 20-25 minutes, till they start to turn a pale golden colour.

Light rye sourdough bread

Pungent in flavour and with a close-textured crumb, this is our much-loved sourdough bread. Shipton Mill light rye flour is a refined type of rye flour. If it is not available, use dark rye flour, or a mixture of half and half dark rye flour and plain white flour.

V, DF, WF

For the rye starter (or 'mother'):
    A handful of rye flour *(light or dark)*
    Water

For the sourdough bread:
    600g / 1 lb 6 oz Shipton Mill light rye flour
    1½ level tsp salt
    Roughly 100ml / 3 ½ fl oz rye sourdough starter
    300-325ml / 11-12 fl oz water
    A round basket, about 20cm / 8" across

Makes one large round loaf

Begin by getting the starter established. Put the rye flour into a bowl and mix it with enough water to make a creamy paste. Cover it and leave it somewhere warm for a few days. By then it should be full of bubbles and can be transferred to a lidded container in the fridge. (From now on, every time it is used, it can be replenished with more flour and water).

To make the sourdough bread, put the flour and salt into a large bowl. Add the sourdough starter and the water and work it into a sticky dough, kneading it as best as you can (rye dough is not easy to knead). Coat the dough with a little olive oil and cover the bowl with a damp tea towel. Leave it to rise at room temperature for several hours, or overnight.

Generously coat the inside of a round basket with flour. Shape the dough into a ball and place it in the basket. Leave it to rise for 1-2 hours, or till it has grown significantly. Preheat the oven to 200°C (Fan 180°C) / Gas mark 7. Invert the loaf onto a greased, floured baking tray and make four shallow slashes around the edge of the loaf, with a sharp knife. Put it into the oven and bake it for about 45 minutes, turning the oven down to 180°C (Fan 160°C) / Gas mark 6, after the first 15 minutes. When fully baked, the loaf will be lightly coloured and feel hard to the touch.

Variation: For a lighter loaf, replace some or all of the rye flour with plain flour. Make the bread in the same way as you would make the rye sourdough bread. Bread dough made with white flour is much more manageable – less sticky and easier to knead. If you prefer, use a large loaf tin for baking the bread, rather than shaping the dough in a basket and turning it onto a baking tray.

RECIPE INDEX

RECIPE INDEX

SPECIAL DIET CODES

The recipes have been coded to give information about their suitability for special diets, using the following abbreviations:

GF - Gluten free
(free from wheat and other grains containing gluten)

WF - Wheat free
(free from wheat, but not other grains containing gluten, such as oats, barley or rye)

DF - Dairy free
(free from products containing cow's milk)

V - Vegan
(free from eggs and products containing cow's, sheep or goat milk)

ACKNOWLEDGEMENTS

We would like to acknowledge the input of the whole of the Star Anise team, past and present, for helping to develop the recipes in this book. Special thanks to co-founders Milda and Alexandra and to long-standing staff members, Azra, Dan, Alex and Rada.

ABOUT THE AUTHORS

Nicholas Allan is co-founder and managing director of Star Anise Arts Café. He trained at the Concord Institute of Integral Studies in London, where he encountered the ideas of wholefoods and macrobiotics. Since then, he has developed his own approach, in response to a growing need in the local community for good, accessible vegetarian food, that takes into account different diets. He still shares much of the day-to-day cooking at the café.

Rahel Steffen is a classically-trained chef, who studied Culinary Arts at the Birmingham College of Food, as well as English at Edinburgh University. She has previously worked in a wide range of kitchens, from a Michelin Star restaurant to an anthroposophical clinic in the West Midlands. A mother of three, she is currently the in-house baker at Star Anise Arts Café.